11+ English

For GL Assessment

This CGP Practice Book is perfect for children aged 7-8 —
it's a fantastic way to start building the skills they'll need for the GL 11+.

It starts with accessible questions to help them get to grips with the basics,
one topic at a time. Once they're happy with those, there's a selection of mixed-topic
Assessment Tests to introduce them to the style of the real 11+ papers.

We've also included full answers at the back of the book, so marking is a piece of cake!

How to access your free Online Edition

This book includes a free Online Edition to read on your PC, Mac or tablet.
You'll just need to go to cgpbooks.co.uk/extras and enter this code:

3017 3895 1179 9587

By the way, this code only works for one person. If somebody else has used
this book before you, they might have already claimed the Online Edition.

Practice Book – Ages 7-8

with Assessment Tests

How to use this Practice Book

This book is divided into two parts — themed question practice and assessment tests. There are answers and detailed explanations at the back of the book.

Themed question practice

- Each page contains practice questions divided by topic. Use these pages to work out your child's strengths and the areas they find tricky. The questions get harder down each page.
- Your child can use the smiley face tick boxes to evaluate how confident they feel with each topic.

Assessment tests

- The second half of the book contains eight assessment tests, each with a comprehension text and a matching set of questions, as well as a set of questions on grammar, spelling and punctuation. They take a similar form to the real test.
- You can print multiple-choice answer sheets so your child can practise the tests as if they're sitting the real thing — visit cgpbooks.co.uk/11plus/answer-sheets or scan the QR code.
- Use the printable answer sheets if you want your child to do each test more than once.
- If you want to give your child timed practice, give them a time limit of 25 minutes for each test, and ask them to work as quickly and carefully as they can.
- The tests get harder from 1-8, so don't be surprised if your child finds the later ones more tricky.
- Your child should aim for a mark of around 85% (21 questions correct) in each test. If they score less than this, use their results to work out the areas they need more practice on.
- If they haven't managed to finish the test in time, they need to work on increasing their speed, whereas if they have made a lot of mistakes, they need to work more carefully.
- Keep track of your child's scores using the progress chart on the inside back cover of the book.

Published by CGP

Editors:
Claire Boulter, Heather Gregson, Holly Poynton, Jo Sharrock

Contributors:
Alison Griffin, Steve Martin, Alison Mott, Julie Moxon, Tina Ramsden

With thanks to Luke Antieul and Lucy Towle for the proofreading.

With thanks to Jane Ellingham for the copyright research.

ISBN: 978 1 78908 152 7

Printed by Elanders Ltd, Newcastle upon Tyne
Clipart from Corel®

Based on the classic CGP style created by Richard Parsons.

Text, design, layout and original illustrations © Coordination Group Publications Ltd. (CGP) 2018
All rights reserved.

Photocopying this book is not permitted, even if you have a CLA licence.
Extra copies are available from CGP with next day delivery • 0800 1712 712 • www.cgpbooks.co.uk

Contents

Tick off the check box for each topic as you go along.

Section One — Grammar

Parts of Speech 2
Verbs 4
Mixed Grammar Questions 6

Section Two — Punctuation

Starting and Ending Sentences 8
Commas 9
Apostrophes 10
Inverted Commas 12
Mixed Punctuation Questions 14

Section Three — Spelling

Plurals 16
Homophones 17
Prefixes and Suffixes 18
Awkward Vowels 19
Awkward Consonants 20
Mixed Spelling Questions 21

Section Four — Writers' Techniques

Alliteration and Onomatopoeia 23
Synonyms 24
Antonyms 25

Section Five — Writing

Creative Writing 26
Non-Fiction Writing 28

Assessment Tests

Test 1 30
Test 2 35
Test 3 40
Test 4 45
Test 5 50
Test 6 55
Test 7 60
Test 8 65

Glossary 70
Answers 71

Section One — Grammar

Parts of Speech

Nouns

Underline the noun in each sentence. For example:

The old black <u>cat</u> yawned loudly.

1. We saw a gorgeous rainbow.

2. The alien stared as I cycled away.

3. I love riding my tiny donkey.

4. He remembered that his puppy barked loudly.

5. She has so many toys that she never knows which to play with.

6. We hoped that she would be OK after the accident.

/ 6

Nouns

Underline the proper noun in each sentence, and write it out with a capital letter. For example:

My sister <u>samia</u> loves dressing up as a monkey. _____Samia_____

7. My family is from scotland. _____

8. I live in a small town in hampshire. _____

9. I've always loved my surname, which is poppleton. _____

10. My brother is starting a new school, garthorpe, next month. _____

11. We're going on holiday in august. _____

12. On tuesday evenings, I go to a gymnastics class. _____

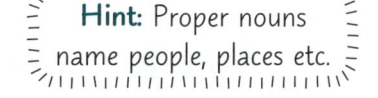

/ 6

Parts of Speech

Pronouns

Write the correct pronoun to replace the words in bold. For example:

My mum's car broke down so **my mum** got home late. _____she_____

1. My friends and I went shopping and **my friends and I** bought a dog. _____

2. Your dad is really good at dancing and **your dad** can sing too. _____

3. Polly draws pictures and **Polly** won first prize in a competition. _____

4. The workers were messing around so the boss told **the workers** off. _____

5. The children weren't sure where **the children** were going. _____

6. We played frisbee and **frisbee** was really fun. _____   / 6

Hint: Read the sentence aloud with your new pronoun in to make sure it sounds right.

Adjectives

Underline the adjective in each sentence. For example:

The captain steered the <u>damaged</u> ship to safety.

7. The boys sneaked up the path to the creepy house.

8. Kit ran to the park to see the exciting funfair.

Hint: Adjectives describe nouns.

9. Ashwin was delighted when he won the trophy.

10. The kind lady gave us directions into town.

11. The jockey had a serious fall from his horse.

12. My rabbit is called Mr Fluffles because he is furry.   / 6

Section One — Grammar

Verbs

Verbs — Underline the verb in each of these sentences. For example:

Jimi <u>ran</u> all the way to school.

1. The pirates sailed their ship through the rough seas.

2. Albert ate an enormous plate of cabbage.

3. My baby sister crawls all over the place.

4. The wicked witch sang a song to the small boy.

5. He asked for another piece of paper.

6. Katy and Chow are on the swings.

Hint: Verbs are doing words like 'sings' or being words like 'is'.

/ 6

Verbs — For each sentence, rewrite the verb in bold in the present tense. For example:

Hari **got** home late from school. _____gets_____

7. I **dressed** my little sister in a red jumper. _____

8. My friends **were** all taller than me. _____

9. John **had** never been to the seaside before. _____

10. My pet frog Hoppy **jumped** really high. _____

11. He **knew** how to do this question. _____

12. The children **talked** during every lesson. _____

Hint: The present tense describes something that is happening now.

/ 6

Section One — Grammar

Verbs

Underline the correct form of the verb to make the sentence past tense. For example:

Fatima (hopes <u>hoped</u> hope) the test wouldn't be too hard.

1. Bettina (**loved love loves**) her brand-new purple shoes.

2. I (**go goes went**) home early because I was ill.

3. My uncle was (**blew blown blows**) over by the helicopter.

4. Naseem (**buy buys bought**) some new watercolour paints.

5. Gemma (**takes took take**) the bus to school today.

6. The flock of geese (**rose rise risen**) into the air.

/ 6

For each sentence, rewrite the verb in bold in the past tense. For example:

Jan **plays** the flute really well.   <u>played</u>

Hint: Often you add '-ed' to the end of a verb to make it past tense, but watch out for verbs where you have to do something different.

7. I **decide** to try the spinach ice cream.   _____

8. We **drink** lemonade during the summer holidays.   _____

9. The fat duck **breaks** the ice in the pond.   _____

10. Daniel **throws** the beanbag high in the air.   _____

11. Kiri **catches** the ball easily with one hand.   _____

12. I **think** I would like to be an actor.   _____

/ 6

Section One — Grammar

Mixed Grammar Questions

Underline the word in each sentence which matches the part of speech in brackets. For example:

Richie <u>sprinted</u> to the bus stop. **(verb)**

Hint: Read each sentence through before you underline your answer.

1. The grumpy old dog snoozed until we woke him. **(noun)**

2. The friendly waitress brought us the drinks. **(adjective)**

3. Marco demanded extra marshmallows on his hot chocolate. **(verb)**

4. The night was dark, but Kerry walked home anyway. **(adjective)**

/ 4

5. The old lady wished she was back at home. **(pronoun)**

6. We sang really loudly for the entire car journey. **(verb)**

7. I'm going to eat some delicious eggs. **(noun)**

8. My uncle has sad eyes, but they twinkle when he smiles. **(adjective)**

/ 4

9. Cecily came home with us after school today. **(verb)**

10. The ducklings quacked loudly because they wanted some bread. **(pronoun)**

11. These flowers smell wonderful in the evening. **(adjective)**

12. Deeba drove my granny to the airport. **(verb)**

/ 4

Section One — Grammar

Mixed Grammar Questions

> Underline the correct word from the brackets to complete each sentence. For example:
>
> Ed **(doing <u>does</u> do)** tai chi every Wednesday night.

1. We are **(go going gone)** to the zoo during the holidays.

2. Anoukh **(left leaving leave)** the tap running so the bath overflowed.

3. The naughty children thought **(it us they)** had got away with it.

4. Simon is the **(quickness quickly fastest)** runner in our class.

/ 4

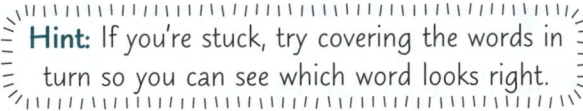

5. My house is **(small smaller smallest)** than Heather's.

6. The brass band **(begin began beginning)** to play as we walked along the beach.

7. The sausages **(burns burning burned)** quickly in the frying pan.

8. The small boys **(were was where)** shouting loudly and excitedly.

/ 4

Hint: If you're stuck, try covering the words in turn so you can see which word looks right.

9. Dad wants **(we us our)** to rent a caravan for our next holiday.

10. Granny **(do done did)** not see the cat until she sat on him.

11. I wish Eduardo would tell me where **(he his they)** is going.

12. Mum was cross when Tom **(break breaks broke)** her favourite mug.

/ 4

Section One — Grammar

Section Two — Punctuation

Starting and Ending Sentences

> Each line contains two sentences. Rewrite each sentence with a capital letter at the start and a full stop at the end. For example:
>
> my dog is called Snuffles he is a poodle
> My dog is called Snuffles. He is a poodle.

1. we are learning French at school it is my favourite subject

2. the pudding looks delicious I wish I hadn't eaten so much mashed potato

3. swimming is really fun we go twice a week

/ 6

> Add a question mark (?) or an exclamation mark (!) to the end of each sentence. For example:
>
> What time will you be home ?

4. Would you rather travel by plane or camel ____

5. Granny has just fallen in the pond ____

6. I can't believe Lois said that ____

Hint: Exclamation marks are sometimes used at the end of sentences to show strong feelings.

7. Do you believe your uncle's story about the foxes ____

8. You'll never eat all that cake ____

9. Where did you see the giant bouncy castle ____

/ 6

Section Two — Punctuation

Commas

Circle the incorrect comma in each sentence. For example:

I bought carrots, pepper**s,** and cheese from the shop.

Hint: Commas can separate extra information in a sentence.

1. We've just got three new rabbits called Bob, Squiggle and, Thump.

2. Last night, my best friend won a singing, competition.

3. The misty, dark and silent forest was especially, creepy at night.

4. I had a sundae with strawberry, vanilla, and mint ice cream.

5. Although Mum said I, could play outside, I was too full after dinner.

6. Despite, the hot and sunny weather, I don't want an ice cream.

/ 6

Put a comma in the correct place in each sentence. For example:

Even though it was cloudy**,** we could still see the moon.

7. I refuse to eat carrots peas and cabbage.

8. Greg Ben and Rob are the tallest boys in our class.

9. Even when it's a school night I stay up late.

10. Although the sun was shining Jacob stayed inside all day.

11. After a game of football I have to wipe the mud off my boots.

12. I taught my parrot to whistle dance and sing.

/ 6

Section Two — Punctuation

Apostrophes

Underline the correct word from the brackets to complete the sentence. For example:

The (butchers <u>butcher's</u>) dog is the size of a horse.

1. My (brothers **brother's**) bedroom has been off-limits since I broke his lamp.

2. The herd of (cows **cow's**) chased us across the field.

3. The (boys **boy's**) sent a package to their pen friends.

Hint: Apostrophes can show that something belongs to someone.

4. Our (cars **car's**) horn is broken because I pressed it too much.

5. The (pupils **pupil's**) all made hats for Victorian Day.

Rewrite these phrases using apostrophes. For example:

the bike belonging to Heidi
<u>Heidi's bike</u>

6. the shop belonging to Mr Dhimar
_____

7. the book belonging to Aidan
_____

8. the coat belonging to the girl
_____

9. the frisbees belonging to the dog
_____

10. the gardens belonging to Mrs Holden
_____

Apostrophes

Rewrite the words in bold using an apostrophe to make their shortened form. For example:

They are going to be here soon. ____They're____

Hint: Remember, the apostrophe goes in the place of the missing letters.

1. **I will** think about your comments. _____

2. That **is not** my tortoise. _____

3. I have no idea why **you are** laughing. _____

4. My friends **have not** seen my pet snake. _____

5. **I am** the thumb-wrestling champion. _____

6. I love my gran because **she is** always nice to me. _____

/ 6

Rewrite the words in bold in their full form, without the apostrophe. For example:

I'm going to give the cat her dinner. ____I am____

7. **We're** going out whether it's raining or not. _____

8. **There's** a pig in the muddy field. _____

9. I **hadn't** expected to see Caroline today. _____

10. When you go out, **you'll** need an umbrella. _____

11. **Don't** stay up too late. You need sleep. _____

12. I **couldn't** smell Paul's sock drawer. _____

/ 6

Section Two — Punctuation

Inverted Commas

Speech

Use either 'said' or 'asked' to complete each sentence. For example:

"Can you peel those potatoes?" _____asked_____ Tanya.

Hint: Think about whether the speech is asking a question or making a statement.

1. "There's someone at the door," _____ Jacob.

2. "Where is the telephone please?" _____ the old lady.

3. Svenja _____ , "I don't mind who curls my hair."

4. "Three boys finished the obstacle course," _____ Mike.

5. "Who wants to go next?" _____ Mrs Hutchinson, smiling.

6. "So Captain Snow, where are we?" _____ Johnny.

/ 6

Inverted Commas

Add inverted commas (" ") to complete each sentence. For example:

"I must buy some coconuts," said Nalak.

7. You can't play football in the garden, said Pete.

8. There's a hole in that bucket, noted Dave.

9. Can you mend my bike? asked Kasra.

Hint: Inverted commas always come in pairs — one set either side of the words that are spoken.

10. Aisha laughed and said, I don't know where they are.

11. Come back! they shouted after him.

12. Kirstie looked worried when she said, Oh dear.

/ 6

Section Two — Punctuation

Inverted Commas

Rewrite these sentences using inverted commas. For example:

> I said, There's Jamie. He's running up the hill.
> I said, "There's Jamie. He's running up the hill."

Hint: Remember to put the right punctuation inside the inverted commas.

1. You haven't tidied up! shouted Dad.

2. Bernard said, I give up.

3. Rahim called, Come on. Let's go!

4. We can't find it anywhere, they said.

/ 4

In each sentence there is a capital letter missing. Draw a circle around the letter which should be a capital. For example:

> I asked, "(h)ow much are those shorts?"

5. "let's stroke the lambs," suggested Becky.

6. Ritu said, "you're not allowed to go alone."

7. "we're going to be late again," said Mum.

8. He called out, "hurry up everybody!"

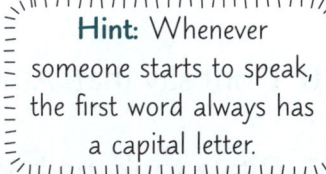

Hint: Whenever someone starts to speak, the first word always has a capital letter.

9. "our school uniform is horrid," I complained to Marieke.

10. Uncle Billy exclaimed, "look! Those people are riding camels!"

/ 6

Section Two — Punctuation

Mixed Punctuation Questions

> Circle the punctuation mistake in each sentence. For example:
>
> Why aren't you⦾ coming to the cinema with us?

1. The old man had dyed his hair,

2. baby Frieda learnt to walk.

3. Get down here?

4. I sleep best when I have a feather Quilt.

5. "Can I go out to play!" asked Ted.

6. Carlos threw the ball "and yelled, "Catch this!"

Hint: Remember all sentences need to start with a capital letter and finish with either a full stop, a question mark or an exclamation mark.

/ 6

> Each of these sentences is missing some punctuation. Draw a circle where the punctuation should be and write the missing punctuation on the line. For example:
>
> Yellow is my favourite colour⦾ **.**

7. two men swam out to the island. ____

8. "Are we nearly there yet? I asked. ____

9. Its nearly time to leave. ____

10. Dont say that, Amy. ____

11. Ritala took the book from the shelf ____

12. When we play football I go in goal. ____

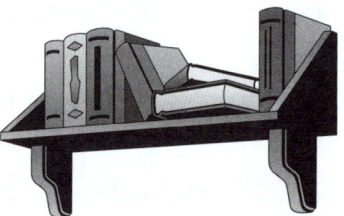

/ 6

Section Two — Punctuation

Mixed Punctuation Questions

Each of these sentences is missing one punctuation mark. Add the missing punctuation mark to each of the sentences. For example:

Do you know where the hotel is **?**

Hint: If you can't see a mistake in a sentence, move on to the next one and come back to it later.

1. " How long are we going for ? asked Hussein .

2. Everybody was at Ben's party except Glenn Sam and Jane .

3. I like eating ice cream , pizza salad and bananas .

4. Before I go to school I clean my teeth.

/ 4

5. " When are you going to tidy your room " asked Dad .

6. Josephine and Hazel are my best friends , " Archna explained .

7. Their dad is an astronaut and he's going to the moon

8. Margarets jacket is the one with the fur hood .

/ 4

9. " Meita " Lesley shouted up the stairs .

10. We're going on a school trip to Germany in the spring .

11. Mum said, " I've got a surprise for you "

12. When I go running I listen to music .

/ 4

Section Three — Spelling

Plurals

Plurals

Write the correct plural of the word in brackets. For example:

Mira and I watched five ___films___ (film).

1. Three _____ (girl) were chosen to carry the flag in the ceremony.

2. The shoes were stacked in _____ (box) on the shelves.

3. We cleaned up the _____ (ash) from the bonfire.

4. My brother has three pairs of _____ (glass) because he always loses them.

5. When we go on holiday I like eating _____ (peach) for breakfast.

6. I blew out the candles on the cake and I made two _____ (wish).

/ 6

Plurals

Underline the correct plural from the brackets to complete the sentence. For example:

The (babys <u>babies</u>) were crying because of the loud noise.

Hint: If there's a consonant before the 'y', drop the 'y' and add 'ies' to make the plural. If there's a vowel before the 'y', just add 's'.

7. Gemma told the **(boys   boyes)** to stop being naughty.

8. The river met at the bottom of three **(vallies   valleys)**.

9. All the **(jellies   jellys)** slid off the table and onto the floor.

10. We couldn't decide which of the **(puppys   puppies)** we wanted to take home.

11. Shing looked across at the **(chimneys   chimnies)** on the roof.

12. There were three **(flys   flies)** caught in the spider's web.

/ 6

Section Three — Spelling

Homophones

Choose the correct homophone from the brackets.
For example:

I have ___to___ (to two too) go to rugby practice now.

Hint: Homophones are words that sound the same but mean different things.

1. Ow! This soup is _____ (to two too) hot.

2. Jamila has _____ (to two too) pet rabbits.

3. I can't go in because the ghost is _____ (to two too) scary.

4. Can we go _____ (to two too) the cinema instead?

/ 4

5. Can I have another _____ (piece peace) of cake?

6. Granny told us to go upstairs so she could get some _____ (piece peace).

7. Luckily, the plate stayed all in one _____ (piece peace).

8. Now we can have dinner in _____ (piece peace).

/ 4

9. Tolek and Sam have lost _____ (they're their there) coats.

10. I wonder whether _____ (they're their there) hats will blow off.

11. Look at my gerbils, _____ (they're their there) so cute!

12. Dad has parked the car over _____ (they're their there).

/ 4

Section Three — Spelling

Prefixes and Suffixes

Suffixes

Add the suffix **ness** or **ship** to complete the word in bold.
For example:

Your **kind**___ness___ to me has been wonderful.

1. I had caught an **ill**_____ which made my ears turn purple.

2. Even though we argue, my sister and I have a good **relation**_____.

3. I've started going roller-blading to improve my **fit**_____.

4. The parents questioned the **fair**_____ of the class test.

5. Amanda has a gym **member**_____ which she never uses.

6. Flavel and Gregson are a perfect ice-skating **partner**_____.

/ 6

Hint: Prefixes and suffixes are groups of letters that can be added to the beginning or end of a word to change its meaning.

Prefixes

Add the prefix **dis**, **im** or **un** to complete the word in bold.
For example:

The banana-shaped hammer was quite ___im___**practical**.

7. There was an _____**pleasant** smell coming from the hallway.

8. Hadi and I _____**agreed** on what the best pudding would be.

9. I was so excited to _____**wrap** the presents.

10. Sometimes my P.E. kit just seems to _____**appear**.

11. The rug was _____**perfect** because I lost count when I was knitting it.

12. The 1,000 piece jigsaw puzzle seemed _____**possible** to complete.

Hint: Read the word in bold with 'dis', 'im' and 'un' in front and see which sounds best.

/ 6

Section Three — Spelling

Awkward Vowels

Vowels — Add a vowel to form the words in bold correctly. For example:

The **j_e_wels** were stolen from the museum last night.

1. When I broke my wrist I was in a lot of **pa____n**.

2. There are sixty **min____tes** in every hour.

3. There's a mysterious creature living in the dark **for____st**.

4. Mumtaz stood looking in the **mirr____r** for hours and hours.

5. When I was at **prim____ry** school, we wore a green uniform.

6. The **po____m** Mum read to me was funny.

Hint: Vowels are the letters 'a', 'e', 'i', 'o' and 'u'.

/ 6

Vowels — Underline the correct word from the brackets to complete each sentence. For example:

The cows had escaped from the (feild <u>field</u>).

Hint: Remember the rule — 'i before e, except after c but only when it rhymes with bee', but don't forget that there are a few words that don't follow this rule.

7. They found an ancient Roman **(shield sheild)** in the ground.

8. Swimming 30 lengths of the pool was a great **(achievement acheivement)**.

9. Aunty Ellen wrote me a **(breif brief)** note to go with the recipe she sent.

10. The **(ceiling cieling)** was covered in pink goo after the pudding exploded.

11. Kushi loves **(science sceince)** because she thinks experiments are fun.

12. I have a **(neice niece)** called Ruthie who likes to run around.

/ 6

Section Three — Spelling

Awkward Consonants

Add the silent letter to form the word in bold correctly. For example:

The __h__ **onest** child said she hadn't taken the jigsaw puzzle.

Hint: Consonants are any letters other than 'a', 'e', 'i', 'o' or 'u'.

1. My brother has a scar which goes across his _____**nuckles**.

2. Caroline's car is **w**_____**ite** so it gets dirty very easily.

3. Dad has some _____**rinkles** around his eyes, which he complains about.

4. I sighed when Grandma said she was _____**nitting** me another woolly hat.

5. Mrs Aboud's garden is full of garden _____**nomes**.

6. We played snakes and ladders for three _____**ours**.

/ 6

Underline the correct word from the brackets to complete each sentence. For example:

You need a (sadle <u>saddle</u>) to ride a horse.

7. Grey (**squirrels** **squirels**) are more common than red ones.

8. Maurice was trying to stop (**biting** **bitting**) his nails.

9. Look at those (**bubles** **bubbles**) coming out of the bathroom.

10. I don't like going (**running** **runing**) in the rain.

11. Nora (**waddles** **wadles**) like a duck when she walks.

12. We were (**hopping** **hoping**) to finish the play before bedtime.

/ 6

Section Three — Spelling

Mixed Spelling Questions

Underline the correct word to complete each sentence. For example:

I was (shakeing <u>shaking</u>) with nerves before I got up to sing.

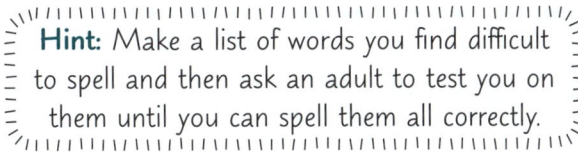

Hint: Make a list of words you find difficult to spell and then ask an adult to test you on them until you can spell them all correctly.

1. I was so **(dishappy unhappy)** when the cricket match was cancelled.

2. We knew the address was **(correct corect)** because Lola had written it carefully.

3. There were **(ditches ditchs)** on both sides of the track.

4. They used the secret **(nock knock)** but no one was in.

/ 4

5. Kevin is **(hideing hiding)** behind the armchair.

6. The **(keys keyes)** for our cottage were left under a flower pot.

7. Uncle Niito taught me how to make **(shado shadow)** puppets.

8. I always try to be **(cheerful cheerfull)**, even if I feel grumpy.

/ 4

9. **(Tomorow Tomorrow)** evening is the final of the cooking challenge.

10. In our garden, we have a tree which grows lots of **(plums plumbs)**.

11. The **(skies skys)** over the countryside are often blue.

12. Our class had enjoyed dressing up as **(aleins aliens)** for the day.

/ 4

Section Three — Spelling

Mixed Spelling Questions

> Underline the word that contains a spelling mistake in each line.
> For example:
>
> Jenna is <u>makeing</u> a patchwork quilt.

1. My freind Leila has beautiful dark hair.

2. We did all the activitys on offer.

3. Miles has court the measles.

4. I accidentally put the sweet rapper in my mouth.

5. My mum always wants to put ribons in my hair.

6. Callum lisened carefully to the music.

/ 6

> Each sentence contains a spelling mistake. Underline the word with the error and write the correct spelling on the line. For example:
>
> The <u>tigar</u> chased after the monkey. _____tiger_____

7. I had hidden Mohab's pensil under the table. _____

8. My uncle Mark is always very joly at Christmas. _____

9. She pulled a small peice of paper out of the hat. _____

10. Tina was only pasing through so she didn't stay. _____

11. I love it when we have pancakes for brekfast. _____

12. We all carried torchs in the Bonfire Night parade. _____

/ 6

Section Three — Spelling

Section Four — Writers' Techniques

Alliteration and Onomatopoeia

Alliteration

Circle the letter that is repeated at the beginning of the most words in each sentence and then write this letter on the line. For example:

A (t)ruly (t)errible (t)ank (t)ore past (t)own. _t_

Hint: Alliteration is when a sound is repeated at the beginning of words in a sentence.

1. Betty put a bit of butter in her batter. _____

2. Summer is the season when we see the sun. _____

3. Fiona found Flora's friend's feather duster. _____

4. The desperate dog ducked under the door. _____

5. Lying on the log, the lazy ladybird laughed. _____

6. Colin came outside to collect the clay. _____

/ 6

Onomatopoeia

Choose an onomatopoeic word from below to fill the gap in each sentence. Each word is only used once. For example:

gulped   clunked   roared   slurped   cooing   popped   ~~screeched~~

The child __screeched__ at the top of her voice.

7. The lid _____ off the cola bottle.

8. I woke up because the doves were _____.

Hint: Onomatopoeic words sound like the noise they describe.

9. The train _____ slowly along the tracks.

10. When Rachel realised she was late, she _____ down her orange juice.

11. Jennie _____ her spaghetti when she was having dinner.

12. The aeroplane _____ over the house.

/ 6

Section Four — Writers' Techniques

Synonyms

Underline the word that has the most similar meaning to the word in bold. For example:

thin   wide   <u>skinny</u>   tall

1. **kind**   mean   blonde   nice

2. **dangerous** raw   safe   risky

3. **happy**   sad   cheerful   cross

4. **noisy**   loud   silent   peaceful

5. **boiling**   cold   wet   hot

6. **windy**   shady   sunny   breezy

Hint: Words with very similar meanings are called synonyms.

/ 6

Underline the word from the brackets that has the most similar meaning to the word in bold. For example:

The kitten was **small**. (large <u>tiny</u> big)

7. I ran really **quickly** up the stairs. (slowly sleepily rapidly)

8. In the winter, it's nice to lie under a warm **quilt**. (sofa blanket curtain)

9. There were lots of **plants** in the garden. (leaves twigs flowers)

10. Marina felt **scared** when she saw the rhino appear. (afraid happy excited)

11. The car was **filthy** after we drove through the field. (dirty clean broken)

12. I wore my **coat** because it was snowing. (skirt jacket hat)

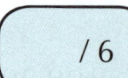

/ 6

Antonyms

Antonyms

Underline the word that has the opposite meaning to the word in bold. For example:

old   hairy   blue   <u>young</u>

1. **neat**   old   shiny   messy

2. **above**   top   under   outside

3. **girl**   boy   friend   neighbour

4. **wide**   inside   narrow   small

5. **busy**   whisper   windy   quiet

6. **expensive** sold   new   cheap

Hint: Antonyms are words that mean the opposite of each other.

/ 6

Antonyms

Underline the word from the brackets that has the opposite meaning to the word in bold. For example:

I have always been scared of the **dark**. (<u>light</u> night moon)

7. The chair was really **soft**. (good easy hard)

8. The box of books is very **heavy** so I can't lift it. (light big high)

9. We went to the wishing well to **fill** a bucket of water. (make empty give)

10. Mum told me I had to **remember** to go to badminton club. (leave forget visit)

11. I never **win** in running races because I'm so slow. (hop go lose)

12. People stare at my dog because he is so **ugly**. (short handsome furry)

/ 6

Section Five — Writing

Creative Writing

Adjectives

Replace the word in bold with a more interesting adjective. For example:

The hat looked **good**. ___fantastic___

1. Phil was **sad** when he failed his flute exam. _____

2. My friend Li is a really **nice** boy. _____

3. The Smiths live in a **big** house. _____

4. I could feel that my face had gone bright **red**. _____

5. Meryn comes from a **small** village in Wales. _____

6. The yard was **wet** after the storm. _____

/ 6

Verbs

Write an interesting verb to complete each sentence. For example:

Mr Domingo ___jumped___ out of his chair when the phone rang.

7. I feel nervous when Juliet _____ at us.

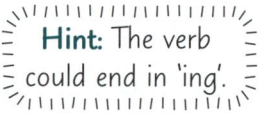
Hint: The verb could end in 'ing'.

8. Gita was very sorry for _____ my glasses.

9. Yesterday, Rosemary and Marik _____ Joe on the arm to wake him up.

10. Carl and Martha _____ merrily as they walk down the road.

11. We _____ out to the car because we knew we would be late.

12. My great uncle Gary likes _____ model aeroplanes.

/ 6

Creative Writing

Adjectives

Adjectives make your stories more detailed. Write two adjectives to describe these characters and places. For example:

A castle ____huge____ ____ruined____

Hint: Try to think of the most interesting words that could describe each thing.

1. A cat _____ _____

2. A policeman _____ _____

3. A witch _____ _____

4. The seaside _____ _____

5. A fairground _____ _____

/ 5

Write a short story that uses two characters and one place from the exercise above. Try to include as many adjectives as possible. Use an extra sheet of paper if you need to.

6. Beginning:
_____
_____
_____

Middle:
_____
_____
_____

End:
_____
_____
_____

/ 6

Section Five — Writing

Non-Fiction Writing

> Read these sentences and write down whether they would be found in a fiction text (F) or a non-fiction text (N). For example:
>
> Canada is the second largest country in the world.   **N**

Hint: Fiction is the word for stories that are made-up, and non-fiction is the word for writing about real things.

1. The moon winked at us and began to sing a lullaby.   _____

2. I opened the door and saw the magical kingdom.   _____

3. Add the eggs and stir the mixture until it is smooth.   _____

4. Frogs have very powerful legs and webbed feet.   _____

5. The monkey jumped into the air and began to speak.   _____

6. Alexander Graham Bell invented the telephone.   _____

/ 6

> Write the correct form of the word or words in brackets to turn each sentence into an instruction. For example:
>
> ____**Fill**____ **(I filled)** the kettle with water.

7. _____ **(I turned)** the light off in the living room.

8. _____ **(I plugged)** in the radio to listen to the show at eight o'clock.

9. _____ **(I fixed)** the picture to the wall in the hallway.

10. _____ **(I took)** bus number six into town.

11. _____ **(I went)** out of the building by the back door.

12. _____ **(I left)** before the end of the party.

/ 6

Non-Fiction Writing

> Write five instructions for each of the following tasks. Write the instructions in the right order and use a new line for each instruction. The first one has been done for you.

1. How to brush your teeth:

   Find your toothbrush and toothpaste.
   _____
   _____
   _____
   _____
   _____
   _____

   / 4

   Hint: Try to write clearly in short sentences and use a new sentence for each new instruction.

2. How to wrap a birthday present:

   Choose some wrapping paper.
   _____
   _____
   _____
   _____
   _____
   _____

   / 4

Section Five — Writing

Assessment Test 1

This book contains eight assessment tests, which get harder as you work through them to help you improve your English skills.

Allow 25 minutes to do each test and work as quickly and as carefully as you can.

If you want to attempt each test more than once, you will need to print **multiple-choice answer sheets** for these questions from our website — go to cgpbooks.co.uk/11plus/answer-sheets or scan the QR code on the right. If you'd prefer to answer the questions on the page, just follow the instructions in the question.

> Read this passage carefully and answer the questions that follow.

Recipe for Blackcurrant Ice Cream

You will need: 284 ml of whipping cream
4 eggs
100 g of caster sugar
3 tablespoons of blackcurrant juice

5 1. Separate the yolks from the egg whites and put them into different bowls. (Ask an adult to help you with this.)
   2. Whisk the egg whites until they form stiff white peaks.
   3. Add the sugar one teaspoon at a time while you continue to whisk the egg whites. The mixture will get stiffer as you do this.
10 4. In another bowl, whisk the cream until it is thick.
   5. Add the cream to the egg white mixture.
   6. Beat the egg yolks for a few seconds, and then add them to the egg white and cream mixture.
   7. Add the blackcurrant juice and stir well.
15 8. Put the mixture into a plastic container and then put it in the freezer for at least 12 hours. (You can store it in the freezer for as long as any other ice cream — up to about 3 months.)
   9. When you want to eat your ice cream, remove it from the freezer about ten minutes beforehand to make it easier to serve.
20 10. Serve with lots of fresh blackcurrants and berries.

Answer these questions about the text that you've just read.
Circle the letter that matches the correct answer.

1. What kind of sugar do you need to make this ice cream?

   A Icing sugar
   B Caster sugar
   C Granulated sugar
   D Blackcurrant-flavoured sugar
   E Demerara sugar

2. What is the first thing you must do to the eggs?

   A Put them in separate bowls
   B Whisk them until they form stiff peaks
   C Separate the egg whites from the yolks
   D Add sugar to them
   E Put them in the freezer

3. What happens when you whisk the sugar and the egg whites?

   A The mixture will become lumpy.
   B The mixture will change colour.
   C The mixture will become thinner.
   D The mixture will become thicker.
   E The mixture will become creamy.

4. What should you do to the cream before adding it to the egg white mixture?

   A Whisk it
   B Add sugar to it
   C Add the egg yolks
   D Freeze it
   E Add the juice

/ 4

Carry on to the next question → →

Assessment Test 1

Answer these questions about the text that you've just read.
Circle the letter that matches the correct answer.

5. When should you add the blackcurrant juice?

   A Straight after separating the egg whites and yolks
   B Straight after adding the yolks to the cream and egg white mixture
   C Straight after whisking the cream
   D Before adding the sugar
   E Before beating the egg yolks

6. What is the minimum amount of time the ice cream takes to freeze?

   A 3 months
   B 12 months
   C 3 hours
   D 12 hours
   E 10 minutes

7. The ice cream will be easier to serve if you:

   A take it out of the freezer 12 hours earlier.
   B keep it in a plastic container.
   C put it in a bowl with plenty of fresh berries.
   D take it out of the freezer 10 minutes before you want to eat it.
   E store it in the freezer for 3 months.

/ 3

Assessment Test 1

Answer these questions about the way words and phrases are used in the passage.

8. Which of these words is closest in meaning to "Beat" (line 12)?

   A Spread
   B Add
   C Measure
   D Cook
   E Mix

9. "Whisk the egg whites until they form stiff white peaks" (line 7). What does this mean?

   A Whisk the egg whites until they change colour.
   B Whisk the egg whites until they are thick and hold their shape.
   C Whisk the egg whites until they double in size.
   D Whisk the egg whites until your arms are stiff.
   E Whisk the egg whites even though it's very hard work.

10. Which of the following is closest in meaning to "beforehand" (line 19)?

    A Later
    B In plenty of time
    C Earlier
    D Ago
    E Soon

/ 3

Choose the right word or phrase to fill the gap.
Circle the letter which matches the correct word.

11. Kai and Luke didn't **arrive** **arriving** **leaves** **arrived** **left** in time for the start of
                          A   B   C   D   E

12. the show. Lots of people **turning** **turned** **turn** **turns** **spin** around as they tried
                                A   B   C   D   E

13. to creep quietly into the theatre. They **can** **did** **had** **was** **do** almost reached
                                              A   B   C   D   E

14. their seats **when** **because** **if** **of** **or** Luke tripped over something in the dark.
                  A   B   C   D   E

15. He fell **above** **under** **between** **over** **beside** , making a huge crashing sound!
              A   B   C   D   E

/ 5

Carry on to the next question → →

Assessment Test 1

> In each sentence, there is one spelling mistake. Circle the letter which matches the part of the sentence with the mistake.

16. It was about time / for the children / to meet there / leader in / the playground.
    A / B / C / D / E

17. Makeing / pancakes is such fun, / especially when / you flip them / in the frying pan.
    A / B / C / D / E

18. When the whether / turned warmer, / they knew that / his garden / would be colourful.
    A / B / C / D / E

19. The hiking group / needed to be / in single file / when walking along / the mudy footpath.
    A / B / C / D / E

20. Jo's mother bought / bright pink winter / gloves for / the whole family / in the sails.
    A / B / C / D / E

/ 5

> In each sentence, there is one punctuation mistake. Circle the letter which matches the part of the sentence with the mistake.

21. After the event, / and before / the presentation, / the crowd were told / that they could'nt leave.
    A / B / C / D / E

22. When "is your / next novel / coming out?" / Karl asked the writer / of his favourite book.
    A / B / C / D / E

23. The crumpet's / were delicious / and they / tasted even better / with homemade raspberry jam.
    A / B / C / D / E

24. "Stop running!" / shouted the / old man as / the children / rushed into Green Park."
    A / B / C / D / E

25. Mr Ramana, / had spades, / trowels, / brooms and other / gardening tools in his shed.
    A / B / C / D / E

/ 5

Total / 25

End of Test

Assessment Test 1

Assessment Test 2

Allow 25 minutes to do this test and work as quickly and as carefully as you can.

You can print **multiple-choice answer sheets** for these questions from our website — go to cgpbooks.co.uk/11plus/answer-sheets or scan the QR code on the right. If you'd prefer to answer the questions on the page, just follow the instructions in the question.

Read this passage carefully and answer the questions that follow.

An Uneasy End to a Walk

Helen folded up her map and looked across the lake in despair. She and Jack were nearing the end of a long lakeside walk from their campsite. The long, hot afternoon was slowly turning cooler and they were tired. In the distance they could see the last ferry of the day. They had planned to catch it to travel back
5   to their campsite at the other end of the lake. If they missed it, they would have to walk all the way back. The walk had taken them several hours and if they had to retrace their steps, it would be dark before they returned. Yet the ferry still looked some way off.

"Come on, Helen," Jack urged her. "If we really hurry, we can manage this.
10   But we'll have to go without an ice cream."

"I don't mind that — so long as we get back!" replied Helen.

They started to run. It wasn't easy as they had rucksacks on their backs containing the remains of a picnic lunch, the map and their waterproofs. Every so often they would have to clamber over a rock or step around a muddy puddle.
15   Neither of them dared to look at their watches, they just kept going.

As they rounded the final corner, they saw to their relief that the ferry was still at the jetty. They dashed towards it, Jack in the lead. As Helen's back foot touched the top step onto the ferry, the ferry attendant blew his whistle and locked the door behind them. They had made it with seconds to spare!

Carry on to the next question → →

Answer these questions about the text that you've just read. Circle the letter that matches the correct answer.

1. The walk in this story was:

    A up a mountain.
    B along a riverbank.
    C by a lake.
    D through a campsite.
    E along a road.

2. When does this story take place?

    A In the morning
    B At lunchtime
    C In the dark
    D In the late afternoon
    E At sunrise

3. Where was Helen and Jack's campsite?

    A At the side of the lake
    B At the edge of a town
    C In the woods
    D Beside the road
    E In a rocky area

4. Why did Helen and Jack find it difficult to run?

    A They had forgotten their trainers.
    B Helen twisted her ankle.
    C They were not very fit.
    D They were carrying rucksacks.
    E The ground was slippery.

/ 4

Assessment Test 2

Answer these questions about the text that you've just read.
Circle the letter that matches the correct answer.

5. Which of the following did Helen and Jack not take on their walk?

   A Food
   B A watch
   C A map
   D Waterproof clothing
   E A picnic blanket

6. What did Helen and Jack try to avoid when they ran to catch the ferry?

   A Rocks
   B Puddles
   C Wild animals
   D Other people
   E Plants

7. What happens at the end of the story?

   A Helen and Jack missed the ferry.
   B Helen and Jack stopped for an ice cream.
   C Helen fell over.
   D Jack caught the ferry, but not Helen.
   E They both caught the ferry.

Carry on to the next question → →

Answer these questions about the way words and phrases are used in the passage.

8. Helen "looked across the lake in despair" (line 1). This means that:

   A she had given up hope of catching the ferry.
   B she was upset by what she saw.
   C she was crying.
   D she was very happy.
   E she was using binoculars to see.

9. Which of these phrases is closest in meaning to "retrace their steps" (line 7)?

   A Find a new route home
   B Walk twice as far as they had before
   C Walk back the way they had come
   D Ask for directions
   E Walk side by side

10. Which of these phrases is closest in meaning to "to their relief" (line 16)?

    A They were disappointed.
    B They were confused.
    C They were surprised.
    D They were pleased.
    E They were concerned.

/ 3

Choose the right word or phrase to fill the gap.
Circle the letter which matches the correct word.

11. Last Friday, we went to **seen** **saw** **see** **sees** **seeing** our new house. Whenever
                             A   B   C   D   E

12. I see it, I **had** **getting** **have** **has** **get** so excited about living there. The house is
               A   B   C   D   E

13. near the town centre, next **by** **to** **near** **of** **on** my favourite restaurant. I hope
                                A   B   C   D   E

14. we will **ate** **eats** **eating** **eaten** **eat** there all the time! The house
             A   B   C   D   E

15. **when** **why** **who** **that** **while** we're moving to has a garden and a terrace too.
     A   B   C   D   E

/ 5

Assessment Test 2

In each sentence, there is one spelling mistake. Circle the letter which matches the part of the sentence with the mistake.

16. Cho's pencill case contained a set of crayons that her favourite aunt had sent her.
    A   B   C   D   E

17. The creem material was not ideal for making the curtains for the twins' bedroom.
    A   B   C   D   E

18. When Molly spotted the circcus clowns, she squealed loudly and made her uncle jump.
    A   B   C   D   E

19. On Friday at about six o'clock, the freinds met at the library to use the computers there.
    A   B   C   D   E

20. The two boys teased their younger sister when she finally returned from the hairdressor.
    A   B   C   D   E

/ 5

In each sentence, there is one punctuation mistake. Circle the letter which matches the part of the sentence with the mistake.

21. we listened to today's weather forecast on the radio and then set off for Plymouth.
    A   B   C   D   E

22. When we get to the Station, we'll buy our tickets for both parts of the journey.
    A   B   C   D   E

23. Two of the city's football teams will play a match for charity at the end of the week?
    A   B   C   D   E

24. Why can't the daffodil's and primroses be packed in the same boxes as the tulips?
    A   B   C   D   E

25. "Dont forget to take your kit with you!" called Mrs Rai loudly across the street.
    A   B   C   D   E

/ 5

Total / 25

End of Test

Assessment Test 2

Assessment Test 3

Allow 25 minutes to do this test and work as quickly and as carefully as you can.

You can print **multiple-choice answer sheets** for these questions from our website — go to cgpbooks.co.uk/11plus/answer-sheets or scan the QR code on the right. If you'd prefer to answer the questions on the page, just follow the instructions in the question.

Read this passage carefully and answer the questions that follow.

First Snow

13 Cliff Road,
Summerton,
YO16 3HU
1st February

5 Dear Badal,

I have missed you very much since I moved to live in England. Everything is new and different. I have so much to tell you!

I was really excited by the thought of living close to the seaside and thought I would be able to play on the beach and swim in the sea everyday. I was wrong!
10 Most of the time when we go to the beach it is so cold and windy that tears run down my cheeks. I wonder if it is ever hot in England.

Anyway, you will never believe what happened. I was shocked when I woke up today and opened my curtains. The garden, trees and the roofs of the houses opposite were white and glittering! My Dad said it is snow and Mum made me
15 wear so many clothes that I couldn't move my arms properly.

I played with the children next door and had so much fun. We built a man out of snow and we sat on a sledge and raced down a hill near our house. Then, we made balls from the snow and hurled them at each other. I will send you some photographs. I really wish you could see the snow.

20   Please write soon and tell me your news.

Love from,
Nisha

Answer these questions about the text that you've just read. Circle the letter that matches the correct answer.

1. Which of these describes where Nisha lives?

   A Near the shops
   B On the beach
   C On a farm
   D In the mountains
   E Near the sea

2. What did Nisha think she would do at the seaside?

   A Collect shells
   B Eat ice cream
   C Walk on the beach
   D Swim in the sea
   E Build sandcastles

3. What does Nisha notice about the temperature in her new country?

   A It is hot.
   B It is sometimes warm.
   C It is never cold.
   D It is very cold.
   E It is quite warm.

4. Why couldn't Nisha move her arms properly?

   A She hurt them when she was throwing snowballs.
   B They were so cold that they went stiff.
   C She had too many clothes on.
   D Her mum told her to keep them still.
   E She was trying not to slip over.

/ 4

Carry on to the next question → →

Assessment Test 3

> Answer these questions about the text that you've just read.
> Circle the letter that matches the correct answer.

5. Where did the children play on their sledges?

    A On the road
    B On a hill
    C On the beach
    D In the garden
    E On a mountain

6. What is Nisha going to send to Badal?

    A Photographs
    B A snowball
    C A postcard
    D An email
    E An invitation to visit her

7. Who did Nisha play with in the snow?

    A Her dad
    B Her sister
    C Her dog
    D The children next door
    E Badal

/ 3

Answer these questions about the way words and phrases are used in the passage.

8. Which phrase from the text tells you that Nisha has not seen Badal for a long time?

    A I was really excited
    B I have missed you
    C Please write soon
    D Everything is new
    E I really wish you could see the snow

9. Which word from the text tells you that Nisha is surprised when she opens the curtains?

    A Snow
    B Shocked
    C Believe
    D Never
    E Happened

10. What does the word "glittering" (line 14) tell you about the snow?

    A It is sparkling.
    B It is deep.
    C It is cold.
    D It is exciting.
    E It is dangerous.

/ 3

Choose the right word or phrase to fill the gap.
Circle the letter which matches the correct word.

11. Billy found the coins in a bag next **on** **by** **from** **of** **to** the hotel. He knew that
                                                                         A B C D E

12. he needed to hand **that's** **they** **there** **their** **them** in to the hotel in case
                                  A   B   C   D   E

13. they belonged to someone. As well **has** **too** **gave** **as** **to** the coins, there was a
                                                    A B C D E

14. beautiful old necklace. When Billy went **on** **over** **into** **down** **up** the hotel lobby,
                                                          A B C D E

15. **they** **he** **she** **we** **you** saw a woman searching the room, as if she'd lost something.
     A   B   C   D   E

/ 5

Carry on to the next question → →

In each sentence, there is one spelling mistake. Circle the letter which matches the part of the sentence with the mistake.

16. Aled tried to open | the back door | of his parents' car | but it seemed | to be frosen shut.
    A | B | C | D | E

17. Nobody could hear | what the visitor | was saying | becuse she spoke | so quietly.
    A | B | C | D | E

18. Colouring and painting | are the | most popular choices | for children | at the holliday club.
    A | B | C | D | E

19. Annie carfully | picked up her | fancy swimming | costume and went | to the changing room.
    A | B | C | D | E

20. Without a | backwards look, | Tommy dashed | along the parth | into the busy street.
    A | B | C | D | E

/ 5

In each sentence, there is one punctuation mistake. Circle the letter which matches the part of the sentence with the mistake.

21. In the wizard's | coat pocket | there was a bus pass, | several small | sea pigs and a pixie
    A | B | C | D | E

22. over by the stream, | the girls opened | their picnic | lunches while | the adults chatted.
    A | B | C | D | E

23. Petra grinned | when she saw | her brother's scooter | and muttered, | "It will be mine"
    A | B | C | D | E

24. Turn left | at the junction, | right before | the Roundabout | and then it's straight ahead.
    A | B | C | D | E

25. During our | last summer holiday's, | we visited | Germany with | two of Philip's cousins.
    A | B | C | D | E

/ 5

Total / 25

End of Test

Assessment Test 3

Assessment Test 4

Allow 25 minutes to do this test and work as quickly and as carefully as you can.

You can print **multiple-choice answer sheets** for these questions from our website — go to cgpbooks.co.uk/11plus/answer-sheets or scan the QR code on the right. If you'd prefer to answer the questions on the page, just follow the instructions in the question.

Read this passage carefully and answer the questions that follow.

A Faithful Friend

Long, long ago, in a land of mountains and valleys, a Prince went hunting in the woods. However, his faithful hound, who usually went with him, was left at the castle.

On his return, the Prince was greeted by his dog. However the animal, who
5 was usually calm and quiet, was barking loudly. Alarmed, the Prince rushed to find his baby son who he had left sleeping upstairs. When he reached the room, the cot was overturned and the baby was nowhere to be seen. "You terrible beast!" the Prince roared. "What have you done?"

In his fury, the Prince instantly commanded his servant to seize the dog and
10 have it banished. The hound was taken away to a distant land where he could not harm the Prince's family again.

As the Prince sat and wept for his child and his lost companion, he thought he heard a baby's cry. Following the sound, the Prince discovered his child behind a cupboard, safe and unharmed. Close by lay the body of an enormous wolf which
15 had been killed by the Prince's faithful hound. In despair the Prince cried, "My good dog, you were protecting my son and yet I have forced you away."

Filled with regret, the Prince travelled to the faraway land where he had banished the dog. He searched for several days until he found the hound, and then brought him back to the palace where the dog protected the Prince and his son for
20 the rest of his life.

Carry on to the next question → →

Answer these questions about the text that you've just read. Circle the letter that matches the correct answer.

1. When did the Prince go out hunting?

    A A windy autumn day
    B Several years ago
    C A long time ago
    D Recently
    E Not very often

2. What happened to the cot?

    A It was broken into pieces.
    B It was knocked over.
    C It was nowhere to be seen.
    D It was hidden.
    E It was behind a cupboard.

3. Which word from the text tells you that the Prince was worried?

    A Alarmed
    B Commanded
    C Roared
    D Barking
    E Fury

4. Why was the dog taken away?

    A Because it had ruined the baby's room.
    B Because it had killed a wolf.
    C Because the Prince thought it had attacked the baby.
    D Because it hadn't gone hunting.
    E Because it had hidden the baby.

/ 4

Assessment Test 4

Answer these questions about the text that you've just read.
Circle the letter that matches the correct answer.

5. Why was the Prince "Filled with regret" (line 17)?

   A The dog had hurt the baby.
   B The dog was well-behaved.
   C The Prince realised he was wrong to blame the dog.
   D The baby was safe.
   E The Prince didn't want to punish the dog.

6. Which statement about the wolf is true?

   A It was huge.
   B It was very hungry.
   C It killed the dog.
   D It didn't like the Prince.
   E It ran away.

7. Which word does not describe what the Prince's dog is like?

   A Evil
   B Brave
   C Loyal
   D Protective
   E Powerful

/ 3

Carry on to the next question → →

Answer these questions about the way words and phrases are used in the passage.

8. Which of these words is closest in meaning to "fury" (line 9)?

   A Excitement
   B Tiredness
   C Joy
   D Sadness
   E Rage

9. What does the word "banished" (line 10) mean?

   A Punished
   B Sent away
   C Locked away
   D Killed
   E Rewarded

10. Which of these words mean the same as "companion" (line 12)?

    A Child
    B Animal
    C Friend
    D Servant
    E Helper

/ 3

Choose the right word or phrase to fill the gap.
Circle the letter which matches the correct word.

11. Tim **drinked** **drank** **drinker** **drink** **drinking** his juice slowly. When his aunt
        A   B   C   D   E

12. said he should **take** **taking** **taken** **takes** **took** a cherry bun, he shook his head.
                    A   B   C   D   E

13. He heard the other children **runner** **runs** **ran** **running** **is running** outside
                                  A   B   C   D   E

14. but he felt too ill to join them. When his aunt **asking** **ask** **asked** **tells** **telling** him
                                                     A   B   C   D   E

15. what was wrong, he didn't answer, except for a shake of **her** **she** **he** **his** **it** head.
                                                              A   B   C   D   E

/ 5

Assessment Test 4

In each sentence, there is one spelling mistake. Circle the letter which matches the part of the sentence with the mistake.

16. The roof of the tent had leeked, soaking their boots and the piles of clothes inside.
       A   B   C   D   E

17. Mandy liked to eat grapes for lunch, but her father usually bought apples and pairs.
       A   B   C   D   E

18. First they stackked the tables in the corner, then they placed the chairs in a huge circle.
       A   B   C   D   E

19. I prefer coffee without milk or suger, but it needs to be incredibly weak and watery.
       A   B   C   D   E

20. As night fell, the team new that they must hurry to reach the building in time.
       A   B   C   D   E

/ 5

In each sentence, there is one punctuation mistake. Circle the letter which matches the part of the sentence with the mistake.

21. "Where's my favourite hat!" demanded Omar as he opened the cupboard in the hallway.
       A   B   C   D   E

22. Paul's cat is brown with white spots but mine's all black and it doesnt have a tail.
       A   B   C   D   E

23. We wanted to buy potatoes, carrots, and onions from her dad's shop in Glasgow.
       A   B   C   D   E

24. At the end of the lesson, Mrs Jones collected everyone's homework about robots
       A   B   C   D   E

25. In december, Thomas and Emilie weren't old enough to go on the ferris wheel.
       A   B   C   D   E

/ 5

Total / 25

End of Test

Assessment Test 4

Assessment Test 5

Allow 25 minutes to do this test and work as quickly and as carefully as you can.

You can print **multiple-choice answer sheets** for these questions from our website — go to cgpbooks.co.uk/11plus/answer-sheets or scan the QR code on the right. If you'd prefer to answer the questions on the page, just follow the instructions in the question.

Read this passage carefully and answer the questions that follow.

Red Squirrels

Red squirrels, which used to be a common sight in Britain, are now becoming increasingly rare. They used to be the only species of squirrel in Europe, but since grey squirrels were brought over from America in the nineteenth century, there are now many more grey squirrels than red squirrels. In Britain, the majority of
5   red squirrels (about 120,000) can be found in Scotland, although there are around 15,000 in England and 3,000 in Wales.

Red squirrels in Britain mainly live in forests and they are well-adapted to living in the treetops, though in other parts of Europe, they live in grassland and desert areas. They can grow to between 18 cm and 24 cm long, with a tail of up to 20 cm
10 which helps the squirrel to balance as it moves through the trees.

Red squirrels do not hibernate over winter, but they spend time in autumn storing food to keep up their strength during the colder months. They collect, and then bury, a wide variety of nuts and seeds. They also eat mushrooms and pine cones and, occasionally, birds' eggs.

15 The nest of a red squirrel is called a drey and is often built in the folds of a tree trunk. Baby squirrels are called kittens and are fed by their mothers until they are about 12 weeks old when they develop their own teeth. Red squirrels usually live for about 3-6 years, but they can live longer in areas where there's lots of food available.

Answer these questions about the text that you've just read.
Circle the letter that matches the correct answer.

1. Where do red squirrels build their nests?

   A In grasslands
   B In deserts
   C In trees
   D In bushes
   E In leaves

2. What are baby squirrels called?

   A Red squirrels
   B Kittens
   C Puppies
   D Dreys
   E Grey squirrels

3. What do squirrels usually do in autumn?

   A Sleep
   B Collect food
   C Make nests
   D Grow thick fur
   E Move to warmer areas

4. According to the passage, what is special about a red squirrel's tail?

   A It helps the squirrel balance.
   B It helps the squirrel move quickly.
   C It helps the squirrel hide from other animals.
   D It helps keep the squirrel warm in winter.
   E It helps the squirrel to build its nest.

/ 4

Carry on to the next question → →

Assessment Test 5

Answer these questions about the text that you've just read.
Circle the letter that matches the correct answer.

5. What happens when baby squirrels are 12 weeks old?

   A They stop eating.
   B They leave the nest.
   C They grow a tail.
   D They grow teeth.
   E They can climb trees.

6. Which of these statements is true?

   A Red squirrels came from America.
   B Grey squirrels used to be a common sight.
   C Grey squirrels came from America.
   D Red squirrels are only found in Britain.
   E Grey squirrels are the only species of squirrel in Europe.

7. According to the passage, which of these do squirrels not eat?

   A Nuts
   B Seeds
   C Pine cones
   D Berries
   E Eggs

/ 3

Assessment Test 5

> Answer these questions about the way words and phrases are used in the passage.

8. What does the word "majority" (line 4) mean?

   A None
   B Half
   C Most
   D Least
   E Fewest

9. What does the word "rare" (line 2) mean?

   A Uncommon
   B Bold
   C Usual
   D Hungry
   E Special

10. What does the word "occasionally" (line 14) mean?

    A Always
    B Sometimes
    C Never
    D Often
    E Usually

/ 3

> Choose the right word or phrase to fill the gap.
> Circle the letter which matches the correct word.

11. Last Sunday, I was **invites** **invite** **inviting** **invited** **invitation** to Yousef's party.
                           A   B   C   D   E

12. His family live next door to my house, so I **see** **sees** **seeing** **saw** **seen** the bright
        A   B   C   D   E

13. red bouncy castle **in** **at** **on** **under** **over** their garden from my window. Yousef's
        A B C D   E

14. mum had made a cake — she had **wrote** **write** **written** **writ** **writed** 'Happy
        A   B   C   D   E

15. Birthday!' on it in icing. Everyone **had** **has** **have** **having** **hadn't** a great time.
        A   B   C   D   E

/ 5

Carry on to the next question → →

Assessment Test 5

In each sentence, there is one spelling mistake. Circle the letter which matches the part of the sentence with the mistake.

16. Both of Jack's eyes nearly poped out of his head as the magic beans began to grow.
    A   B   C   D   E

17. The lonely female zebra trotted over to the herd, swishing her tail to keep the flys away.
    A   B   C   D   E

18. Grinning to herself, the old which hobbled over to the enormous oven and stirred the pot.
    A   B   C   D   E

19. "Well," whispered the gnome, "it's a miracle that you didn't fall in the puddel."
    A   B   C   D   E

20. Penguins, seals and polar bears are often found in the chillyest places on Earth.
    A   B   C   D   E

/ 5

In each sentence, there is one punctuation mistake. Circle the letter which matches the part of the sentence with the mistake.

21. "My full name is Henry Angus MacDonald," said the tiny man" in a squeaky voice.
    A   B   C   D   E

22. "Would you like one of these"? asked the child who was holding out the biscuit.
    A   B   C   D   E

23. Mount Etna is an active, volcano that is located on the east of the island of Scily.
    A   B   C   D   E

24. "Let's go down to the old quarry because theres' a haunted cave," said Misha.
    A   B   C   D   E

25. Even though they had escaped the warlock's Castle, they were still very afraid.
    A   B   C   D   E

/ 5

Total / 25

End of Test

Assessment Test 5

Assessment Test 6

Allow 25 minutes to do this test and work as quickly and as carefully as you can.

You can print **multiple-choice answer sheets** for these questions from our website — go to cgpbooks.co.uk/11plus/answer-sheets or scan the QR code on the right. If you'd prefer to answer the questions on the page, just follow the instructions in the question.

Read this poem carefully and answer the questions that follow.

An Extract from 'You Are Old, Father William'

"You are old, Father William," the young man said,

"And your hair has become very white;

And yet you incessantly* stand on your head —

Do you think, at your age, it is right?"

5   "In my youth," Father William replied to his son,

"I feared it might injure the brain;

But, now that I'm perfectly sure I have none,

Why, I do it again and again."

"You are old," said the youth, "as I mentioned before,

10 And have grown most uncommonly fat;

Yet you turned a back-somersault in at the door —

Pray, what is the reason of that?"

by Lewis Carroll

*incessantly — regularly

Carry on to the next question → →

Answer these questions about the text that you've just read.
Circle the letter that matches the correct answer.

1. Which of these descriptions best fits Father William?

   A Old, pale, fat
   B Young, white-haired, overweight
   C Old, white-haired, thin
   D Old, white-haired, overweight
   E A youth, uncommon, fat

2. In line 4, the young man is asking Father William whether:

   A he is the right age.
   B he should be standing on his head at his age.
   C he should be thinking at his age.
   D he is right to have such white hair.
   E he knows how old he is.

3. According to the passage, how often does Father William stand on his head?

   A Never
   B Sometimes
   C Over and over again
   D On his birthday
   E Every week

4. Why didn't Father William stand on his head when he was younger?

   A He didn't know how to.
   B He was frightened of being upside down.
   C He was so heavy that he fell over.
   D He was worried that he might injure himself.
   E He was too youthful.

/ 4

Assessment Test 6

Answer these questions about the text that you've just read.
Circle the letter that matches the correct answer.

5. Why is Father William confident that he can do headstands now?

   A He has practised a lot and can do perfect handstands.
   B He is old enough to know how to do headstands.
   C He doesn't do headstands very often.
   D He injured his brain because he did so many headstands.
   E He isn't afraid of getting hurt because he thinks he doesn't have a brain.

6. Why is the young man surprised that Father William does somersaults?

   A Because Father William is fat.
   B Because Father William is at the door.
   C Because Father William has white hair.
   D Because Father William has injured his brain.
   E Because Father William does headstands.

7. What is the young man asking in line 12?

   A Why Father William prays
   B Why Father William does somersaults
   C Why Father William is so old
   D Why Father William turns away from the door
   E Why Father William is so strange

/ 3

Carry on to the next question → →

58

> Answer these questions about the way words and phrases are used in the passage.

8. Which of these phrases is closest in meaning to "In my youth" (line 5)?

    A In my childhood
    B In my adult years
    C When I was a baby
    D When I was foolish
    E In the years I was married

9. What does the word "replied" (line 5) mean?

    A Asked
    B Shouted
    C Answered
    D Laughed
    E Thought

10. What does the word "mentioned" (line 9) mean?

    A Screamed
    B Looked
    C Dreamed
    D Tasted
    E Said

/ 3

> Choose the right word or phrase to fill the gap.
> Circle the letter which matches the correct word.

11. I **knew** **knews** **knowing** **knowed** **knewed** it was going to be a bad day when I
       A   B   C   D   E

12. woke up late. When I asked Mum **when** **how** **where** **while** **who** my shirt was,
                                      A   B   C   D   E

13. she said that some **mices** **mouse** **mice** **mouses** **mouse's** had nibbled a hole in
                         A   B   C   D   E

14. it. I got in the shower but it **quick** **quicklier** **quickest** **quickly** **quicker** turned
                                      A   B   C   D   E

15. freezing cold! It was the **more bad** **badder** **worse** **worst** **worser** morning ever.
                                  A   B   C   D   E

/ 5

Assessment Test 6

In each sentence, there is one spelling mistake. Circle the letter which matches the part of the sentence with the mistake.

16. If you'd listend carefully, you might have heard a songbird somewhere in the garden.
    A   B   C   D   E

17. All the little clay animals tumbled off the shelves and crashed onto the woodden floor.
    A   B   C   D   E

18. Sir Arthur was an old night and his knees hurt from many months of marching.
    A   B   C   D   E

19. The fisherman fought with the shark for hours but it finally managed to brake free.
    A   B   C   D   E

20. I know a good butcher in town wear you can get delicious pies and sausages.
    A   B   C   D   E

/ 5

In each sentence, there is one punctuation mistake. Circle the letter which matches the part of the sentence with the mistake.

21. I went to the shop and I bought some frog's, a small toad and a pound of fleas.
    A   B   C   D   E

22. As they passed, through the door, they discovered a dark forest full of strange sounds.
    A   B   C   D   E

23. Did you know that the picture I drew of our canary won first prize in the competition.
    A   B   C   D   E

24. He's stolen my trolley!" yelled the old lady as she shook her walking stick at Fabian.
    A   B   C   D   E

25. Arctic foxes have thick fur and hairy paws to protect them from the bitter, cold.
    A   B   C   D   E

/ 5

Total / 25

End of Test

Assessment Test 6

Assessment Test 7

Allow 25 minutes to do this test and work as quickly and as carefully as you can.

You can print **multiple-choice answer sheets** for these questions from our website — go to cgpbooks.co.uk/11plus/answer-sheets or scan the QR code on the right. If you'd prefer to answer the questions on the page, just follow the instructions in the question.

Read this passage carefully and answer the questions that follow.

The Forest

Tariq decided that it was time to head back to the tent. He had turned around and was walking in the direction he'd come, but the woods looked different now that it was growing dark. The tall black trees looked sinister, as if they had long, spindly arms stretching towards him.

5   He began to run as fast as he could but the woods clawed at his clothes, slapped his face, and tried to trip him up. Was that the wind he could hear in the trees, or was it something stalking him through the woods? He let out a small cry and rushed onwards but suddenly there was nowhere left to run. Before him stood a line of bushes blocking his way forward. He was trapped!

10   Panicking, he charged straight into the dense bushes. The branches and thorns tore at his clothes as if they were trying to prevent him from escaping. Tariq didn't give up. He fought and fought until, suddenly, he fell through to the other side and landed on the ground with a crash!

       "Hi, Tariq. Just in time. Dinner's nearly ready." Dad was standing ten metres
15 away, in front of the tent. He was wearing a ridiculous apron and holding a frying pan in his hand. Tariq didn't know whether to laugh or cry.

Answer these questions about the text that you've just read.
Circle the letter that matches the correct answer.

1. Why did the woods look different to Tariq when he was heading back to the tent?

    A Because night was falling.
    B Because he was lost.
    C Because he was going back a different way.
    D Because he was surrounded by trees.
    E Because he was scared.

2. Which one of these does Tariq not do in the passage?

    A Run
    B Walk
    C Fall over
    D Cry out
    E Crawl

3. Why did the sound of the wind scare Tariq?

    A He thought that he would be caught in a storm.
    B He thought that it might be the sound of something following him.
    C He thought it would whip the branches and thorns in his face.
    D He thought the wind would blow the tent down.
    E It forced him to rush onward.

4. How did Tariq react when he saw the dense bushes?

    A He gave up because he was trapped.
    B He looked along the bushes for a way through.
    C He jumped over them and crashed to the ground.
    D He tripped and fell over.
    E He forced his way through them.

/ 4

Carry on to the next question → →

Assessment Test 7

Answer these questions about the text that you've just read.
Circle the letter that matches the correct answer.

5. Which of the following statements is not true?

   A Somebody slapped Tariq's face.
   B Tariq is frightened.
   C Tariq is camping.
   D Tariq tore his clothes on the thorns.
   E Tariq's dad was close to the tent.

6. Which word best describes how Tariq returns to the campsite?

   A Loudly
   B Quietly
   C Carefully
   D Slowly
   E Gracefully

7. When Tariq returns, what is his father doing?

   A Searching for him
   B Being ridiculous
   C Cooking dinner
   D Putting up the tent
   E Laughing

/ 3

Assessment Test 7

Answer these questions about the way words and phrases are used in the passage.

8. Which of these words is closest in meaning to "clawed" (line 5)?

   A Tickled
   B Tripped
   C Snapped
   D Waved
   E Scratched

9. Which of these words is closest in meaning to "dense" (line 10)?

   A Thick
   B Sharp
   C Scratchy
   D Twisted
   E Scary

10. Which of these words is closest in meaning to "prevent" (line 11)?

    A Help
    B Stop
    C Frighten
    D Annoy
    E Delay

/ 3

Choose the right word or phrase to fill the gap.
Circle the letter which matches the correct word.

11. Josh is one of three brothers who **living** **live** **life** **lifes** **is live** in our village.
                                                     A   B   C   D   E

12. The three brothers **is** **be** **being** **am** **are** always together. They spend every
                               A B   C   D E

13. evening and weekend in **they're** **their** **its** **it's** **there** tree house, planning exciting
                                     A   B   C D   E

14. adventures. You can hear **them** **your** **his** **our** **they** laughing when you go
                                 A   B   C   D   E

15. past **because** **yet** **if** **so** **by** they are having so much fun.
           A   B C D E

/ 5

Carry on to the next question → →

> In each sentence, there is one spelling mistake. Circle the letter which matches the part of the sentence with the mistake.

16. Our neighbours | grow their own | vegetables | in the garden and pick | them buy hand.
    A | B | C | D | E

17. When watching | badgers in the woods, | you must move | quietly so they | can't here you.
    A | B | C | D | E

18. I would like to go | to the seeside | with my friends, | once the summer | holidays have started.
    A | B | C | D | E

19. The wind howled | and the rain poured | as the waves | crashed into | the wite cliffs.
    A | B | C | D | E

20. Tom ate everything | on his plate | because he didn't | want to waist | any of the food.
    A | B | C | D | E

/ 5

> In each sentence, there is one punctuation mistake. Circle the letter which matches the part of the sentence with the mistake.

21. "Please tell your dog | not to eat your | homework again," | said the Teacher | patiently.
    A | B | C | D | E

22. Have you ever been | really embarrassed | and wanted the ground | to swallow | you up.
    A | B | C | D | E

23. As the growling, | grew louder, | I pulled the duvet | over my head | and shut my eyes.
    A | B | C | D | E

24. When it's feeling threatened, | the short-horned lizard | can squirt | blood from | its eyes'.
    A | B | C | D | E

25. "Tidy your room | before you | play football?" | shouted Dad as | he stood in the hallway.
    A | B | C | D | E

/ 5

Total / 25

End of Test

Assessment Test 7

Assessment Test 8

Allow 25 minutes to do this test and work as quickly and as carefully as you can.

You can print **multiple-choice answer sheets** for these questions from our website — go to cgpbooks.co.uk/11plus/answer-sheets or scan the QR code on the right. If you'd prefer to answer the questions on the page, just follow the instructions in the question.

Read this passage carefully and answer the questions that follow.

The Roman Empire

The world has seen many empires rise and fall, but the most famous of all is the Roman Empire. Founded in Italy, the Roman Empire existed about 2000 years ago, and at its peak controlled the lands from western Europe to northern Africa as well as parts of Asia and the Middle East. This meant that everyone who lived
5   in a country which was part of the Roman Empire had to obey Roman laws. Even as the Roman Empire grew bigger, Rome remained the capital city and it was there that many emperors lived.

One of the reasons the Roman Empire was able to defeat so many countries was the fact that it had a strong, organised army. Roman soldiers served in the
10   army for 25 years, so they were experienced warriors. They also had lots of equipment like helmets, shields and spears so they were well prepared for battle.

However, the Romans were famous for more than just their fighting skills. They were also talented builders who built bridges, baths, theatres and temples in the countries that they invaded. They even linked their Empire with a road
15   network which allowed them to transport soldiers and goods quickly and directly. Today, there are plenty of Roman ruins still standing which remind us how powerful the Roman Empire was.

Carry on to the next question → →

> Answer these questions about the text that you've just read.
> Circle the letter that matches the correct answer.

1. According to the text, who had to obey Roman laws?

    A All Roman soldiers
    B Everyone living in Rome
    C Everyone in the Roman Empire
    D All Roman builders
    E Everyone living in Italy

2. According to the text, which of the following was not built by the Romans?

    A Bridges
    B Places of worship
    C Theatres
    D Roads
    E Markets

3. Which of the following is not mentioned in the text?

    A Rome is named after the Roman Empire.
    B The Roman army was strong.
    C The Roman Empire existed 2000 years ago.
    D There are Roman ruins still standing today.
    E The Romans built baths.

4. According to the text, which of the following best describes Roman roads?

    A Narrow
    B Confusing
    C Dusty
    D Direct
    E Long

/ 4

Answer these questions about the text that you've just read.
Circle the letter that matches the correct answer.

5. Why was the Roman army so strong?

   A The soldiers were very rich.
   B The soldiers were well-equipped with weapons and armour.
   C The soldiers had to be over 25 years old to join the army.
   D The soldiers were very good builders.
   E The soldiers were ruled by emperors.

6. Which of these is not mentioned in the text?

   A Emperors
   B Temples
   C Ruins
   D Roads
   E Hospitals

7. According to the text, which of the following was not part of the Roman Empire?

   A The Middle East
   B Parts of Asia
   C North Africa
   D South Africa
   E Western Europe

/ 3

Carry on to the next question → →

Assessment Test 8

Answer these questions about the way words and phrases are used in the passage.

8. Which of these words is closest in meaning to "talented" (line 13)?

    A Rich
    B Wise
    C Honest
    D Friendly
    E Skilful

9. Which of these words is closest in meaning to "remained" (line 6)?

    A Stayed
    B Waited
    C Remembered
    D Forgot
    E Showed

10. Which of these phrases is closest in meaning to "at its peak" (line 3)?

    A At its most powerful
    B At its tallest
    C At its richest
    D At its busiest
    E At its sharpest

/ 3

Choose the right word or phrase to fill the gap.
Circle the letter which matches the correct word.

11. Jo shut the door so that Bob could not **escaped** **escapes** **escaping** **escape** **out** .
                                                    A   B   C   D   E

12. Although it was snowing **heavy** **heaviest** **heavier** **heavily** **move heavy** , the dog
                                      A   B   C   D   E

13. wanted to go for a walk. Jo rubbed her hands **apart** **between** **in** **on** **together**
                                                              A   B   C   D   E

14. and put on an extra jumper **because** **to** **though** **so** **and** try to keep warm. She
                                      A   B   C   D   E

15. brought extra logs to **put** **putting** **putted** **puts** **is putting** on the fire.
                               A   B   C   D   E

/ 5

Assessment Test 8

In each sentence, there is one spelling mistake. Circle the letter which matches the part of the sentence with the mistake.

16. "What would you like in your sandwhiches?" asked Mum, as she opened the fridge.
    A — B — C — D — E

17. Our teacher told us that the blue whale is the biggist creature that exists on Earth.
    A — B — C — D — E

18. Ellen laughed out loud when her brother tripped and fell into the pool of warter.
    A — B — C — D — E

19. The magician quickly closed the lid and disappeared in a large puff of white smocke.
    A — B — C — D — E

20. The young foxs watched as their mother crept closer to the bird's nest.
    A — B — C — D — E

/ 5

In each sentence, there is one punctuation mistake. Circle the letter which matches the part of the sentence with the mistake.

21. Parvati's family had two rabbits, a cat, a hamster, a goldfish, and a newborn puppy.
    A — B — C — D — E

22. Every Sunday afternoon, my dad play's golf with his best friends at our local golf course.
    A — B — C — D — E

23. "I'm just about to order a takeaway pizza!" Dad shouted from the bottom of the stairs."
    A — B — C — D — E

24. The head teacher was very kind to Rose when she forgot her words during assembly
    A — B — C — D — E

25. The snow leopard lives in the Mountains of Asia, but it is very rare.
    A — B — C — D — E

/ 5

Total / 25

End of Test

Assessment Test 8

Glossary

adjective	A word that describes a noun, e.g. "sunny morning", "frosty lawn".
alliteration	The repetition of a sound at the beginning of words within a phrase, e.g. "Loopy Lois likes lipstick."
antonym	A word with the opposite meaning to another word, e.g. "on" and "off".
consonant	All the letters in the alphabet that aren't vowels (see below).
fiction	Text that has been made up by the author, about imaginary people and events.
homophones	Words that sound the same, but mean different things, e.g. "hair" and "hare".
non-fiction	Text that is about facts and real people and events.
noun	A word that names something, e.g. "scissors", "loyalty".
onomatopoeia	When words sound like the noise they describe, e.g. "pop", "bang".
phrase	A small part of a sentence, usually without a verb e.g. "the purple dress".
plural	More than one of something, e.g. "birds".
prefix	Letters that can be put in front of a word to change its meaning, e.g. "unlock".
pronoun	Words that can be used instead of nouns, e.g. "I", "you", "he", "it".
proper noun	A name for a particular place, thing or person, e.g. "James", "Paris". Proper nouns always start with a capital letter.
suffix	Letters that can be put after a word to change its meaning, e.g. "useful".
synonym	A word with a similar meaning to another word, e.g. "big" and "huge".
verb	An action or being word, e.g. "I run", "he went", "we think".
vowel	The letters "a", "e", "i", "o", "u".

Answers

Page 2 — Parts of Speech
1) **rainbow** — 'rainbow' is a noun because it is a naming word.
2) **alien** — 'alien' is a noun because it is a naming word.
3) **donkey** — 'donkey' is a noun because it is a naming word.
4) **puppy** — 'puppy' is a noun because it is a naming word.
5) **toys** — 'toys' is a noun because it is a naming word.
6) **accident** — 'accident' is a noun because it is a naming word.
7) **Scotland** — 'Scotland' is a proper noun because it is a name of a country.
8) **Hampshire** — 'Hampshire' is a proper noun because it is a name of a county.
9) **Poppleton** — 'Poppleton' is a proper noun because it is a surname.
10) **Garthorpe** — 'Garthorpe' is a proper noun because it is the name of a school.
11) **August** — 'August' is a proper noun because it is the name of a month.
12) **Tuesday** — 'Tuesday' is a proper noun because it is the name of a day of the week.

Page 3 — Parts of Speech
1) **we** — 'we' is the correct pronoun to replace 'my friends and I' because it is plural.
2) **he** — 'he' is the correct pronoun to replace 'your dad' because 'dad' is male.
3) **she** — 'she' is the correct pronoun to replace 'Polly' because 'Polly' is female.
4) **them** — 'them' is the correct pronoun to replace 'the workers' because it is plural.
5) **they** — 'they' is the correct pronoun to replace 'the children' because it is plural.
6) **it** — 'it' is the correct pronoun to replace the word 'frisbee' because a frisbee is an object so it isn't male or female.
7) **creepy** — 'creepy' is an adjective because it describes the noun — 'house'.
8) **exciting** — 'exciting' is an adjective because it describes the noun — 'funfair'.
9) **delighted** — 'delighted' is an adjective because it describes how Ashwin felt.
10) **kind** — 'kind' is an adjective because it describes the noun — 'lady'.
11) **serious** — 'serious' is an adjective because it describes the noun — 'fall'.
12) **furry** — 'furry' is an adjective because it describes the rabbit.

Page 4 — Verbs
1) **sailed** — 'sailed' is the verb — it is an action word.
2) **ate** — 'ate' is the verb — it is an action word.
3) **crawls** — 'crawls' is the verb — it is an action word.
4) **sang** — 'sang' is the verb — it is an action word.
5) **asked** — 'asked' is the verb — it is an action word.
6) **are** — 'are' is the verb — it is a being word.
7) **dress** — In the present tense the sentence would be 'I dress my little sister in a red jumper'.
8) **are** — In the present tense the sentence would be 'My friends are all taller than me'.
9) **has** — In the present tense the sentence would be 'John has never been to the seaside before'.
10) **jumps** — In the present tense the sentence would be 'My pet frog Hoppy jumps really high'.
11) **knows** — In the present tense the sentence would be 'He knows how to do this question'.
12) **talk** — In the present tense the sentence would be 'The children talk during every lesson'.

Page 5 — Verbs
1) **loved** — The sentence should be 'Bettina loved her brand-new purple shoes.' This is the correct past tense form of the verb 'to love' and agrees with the noun — 'Bettina'.
2) **went** — The sentence should be 'I went home early because I was ill.' This is the correct past tense form of the verb 'to go' and agrees with the pronoun — 'I'.
3) **blown** — The sentence should be 'My uncle was blown over by the helicopter.' This is the correct past tense form of the verb 'to blow' and agrees with the noun phrase — 'My uncle'.
4) **bought** — The sentence should be 'Naseem bought some new watercolour paints.' This is the correct past tense form of the verb 'to buy' and agrees with the noun — 'Naseem'.
5) **took** — The sentence should be 'Gemma took the bus to school today.' This is the correct past tense form of the verb 'to take' and agrees with the noun — 'Gemma'.
6) **rose** — The sentence should be 'The flock of geese rose into the air.' This is the correct past tense form of the verb 'to rise' and agrees with the noun phrase — 'The flock of geese'.
7) **decided** — The sentence should be 'I decided to try the spinach ice cream.' This is the correct past tense form of the verb 'to decide' and agrees with the pronoun — 'I'.
8) **drank** — The sentence should be 'We drank lemonade during the summer holidays.' This is the correct past tense form of the verb 'to drink' and agrees with the pronoun — 'We'.
9) **broke** — The sentence should be 'The fat duck broke the ice in the pond.' This is the correct past tense form of the verb 'to break' and agrees with the noun phrase — 'The fat duck'.
10) **threw** — The sentence should be 'Daniel threw the beanbag high in the air.' This is the correct past tense form of the verb 'to throw' and agrees with the noun — 'Daniel'.
11) **caught** — The sentence should be 'Kiri caught the ball easily with one hand.' This is the correct past tense form of the verb 'to catch' and agrees with the noun — 'Kiri'.
12) **thought** — The sentence should be 'I thought I would like to be an actor'. This is the correct past tense form of the verb 'to think' and agrees with the pronoun — 'I'.

Page 6 — Mixed Grammar Questions
1) **dog** — 'dog' is the noun in this sentence, it is a naming word.
2) **friendly** — 'friendly' is the adjective in this sentence, it describes the waitress.
3) **demanded** — 'demanded' is the verb in this sentence, it is the doing word.
4) **dark** — 'dark' is the adjective in this sentence, it describes the night.
5) **she** — 'she' is the pronoun in this sentence, it replaces the noun phrase 'the old lady'.
6) **sang** — 'sang' is the verb in this sentence, it is the doing word.
7) **eggs** — 'eggs' is the noun in this sentence, it is a naming word.
8) **sad** — 'sad' is the adjective in this sentence, it describes the uncle's eyes.
9) **came** — 'came' is the verb in this sentence, it is the doing word.

10) **they** — 'they' is the pronoun in this sentence, it replaces the noun phrase 'the ducklings'.
11) **wonderful** — 'wonderful' is the adjective in this sentence, it describes the flowers.
12) **drove** — 'drove' is the verb in this sentence, it is the doing word.

Page 7 — Mixed Grammar Questions

1) **going** — The sentence should be 'We are going to the zoo during the holidays.' This is the correct option to complete the verb phrase 'are going'.
2) **left** — The sentence should be 'Anoukh left the tap running so the bath overflowed.' This is the correct past tense form of the verb 'to leave' and agrees with the noun 'Anoukh'.
3) **they** — The sentence should be 'The naughty children thought they had got away with it.' This is the correct pronoun for 'the naughty children'.
4) **fastest** — The sentence should be 'Simon is the fastest runner in our class.' This is the correct option to complete the sentence.
5) **smaller** — The sentence should be 'My house is smaller than Heather's.' This is the correct option to complete the sentence.
6) **began** — The sentence should be 'The brass band began to play as we walked along the beach.' This is the correct past tense form of the verb 'to begin' and agrees with the noun phrase 'The brass band'.
7) **burned** — The sentence should be 'The sausages burned quickly in the frying pan.' This is the correct past tense form of the verb 'to burn' and agrees with the noun phrase 'The sausages'.
8) **were** — The sentence should be 'The small boys were shouting loudly and excitedly.' This is the correct past tense form of the verb 'to be' and agrees with the noun phrase 'The small boys'.
9) **us** — The sentence should be 'Dad wants us to rent a caravan for our next holiday.' This is the correct pronoun to complete the sentence.
10) **did** — The sentence should be 'Granny did not see the cat until she sat on him.' This is the correct option to complete the phrase 'did not'.
11) **he** — The sentence should be 'I wish Eduardo would tell me where he is going.' This is the correct pronoun for the noun 'Eduardo'.
12) **broke** — The sentence should be 'Mum was cross when Tom broke her favourite mug.' This is the correct past tense form of the verb 'to break' and agrees with the noun 'Tom'.

Page 8 — Starting and Ending Sentences

1) <u>We are learning French at School.</u> <u>It is my favourite subject.</u> — Each sentence should start with a capital letter and end with a full stop. There is a mark for each correct sentence.
2) <u>The pudding looks delicious.</u> <u>I wish I hadn't eaten so much mashed potato.</u> — Each sentence should start with a capital letter and end with a full stop. There is a mark for each correct sentence.
3) <u>Swimming is really fun.</u> <u>We go twice a week.</u> — Each sentence should start with a capital letter and end with a full stop. There is a mark for each correct sentence.
4) **?** — This is a question so it needs a question mark.
5) **!** — This shows strong feelings so it needs an exclamation mark.
6) **!** — This shows strong feelings so it needs an exclamation mark.
7) **?** — This is a question so it needs a question mark.
8) **!** — This shows strong feelings so it needs an exclamation mark.
9) **?** — This is a question so it needs a question mark.

Page 9 — Commas

1) **and, Thump** — The sentence should be 'We've just got three new rabbits called Bob, Squiggle <u>and Thump</u>.'
2) **singing, competition** — The sentence should be 'Last night, my best friend won a <u>singing competition</u>.'
3) **especially, creepy** — The sentence should be 'The misty, dark and silent forest was <u>especially creepy</u> at night.'
4) **vanilla, and** — The sentence should be 'I had a sundae with strawberry, <u>vanilla and</u> mint ice cream.'
5) **I, could** — The sentence should be 'Although Mum said <u>I could</u> play outside, I was too full after dinner.'
6) **Despite, the** — The sentence should be '<u>Despite the</u> hot and sunny weather, I don't want an ice cream.'
7) **carrots, peas** — The sentence should be 'I refuse to eat <u>carrots, peas</u> and cabbage.'
8) **Greg, Ben** — The sentence should be '<u>Greg, Ben</u> and Rob are the tallest boys in our class.'
9) **night, I** — The sentence should be 'Even when it's a school <u>night, I</u> stay up late.'
10) **shining, Jacob** — The sentence should be 'Although the sun was <u>shining, Jacob</u> stayed inside all day.'
11) **football, I** — The sentence should be 'After a game of <u>football, I</u> have to wipe the mud off my boots.'
12) **whistle, dance** — The sentence should be 'I taught my parrot to <u>whistle, dance</u> and sing.'

Page 10 — Apostrophes

1) **brother's** — 'brother's' is correct here — it shows that the bedroom belongs to the brother.
2) **cows** — 'cows' is correct here — it is a plural so it doesn't need an apostrophe.
3) **boys** — 'boys' is correct here — it is a plural so it doesn't need an apostrophe.
4) **car's** — 'car's' is correct here — it shows that the horn belongs to the car.
5) **pupils** — 'pupils' is correct here — it is a plural so it doesn't need an apostrophe.
6) **Mr Dhimar's shop** — The apostrophe shows that the shop belongs to Mr Dhimar.
7) **Aidan's book** — The apostrophe shows that the book belongs to Aidan.
8) **the girl's coat** — The apostrophe shows that the coat belongs to the girl.
9) **the dog's frisbees** — The apostrophe shows that the frisbees belong to the dog.
10) **Mrs Holden's gardens** — The apostrophe shows that the gardens belong to Mrs Holden.

Page 11 — Apostrophes

1) **I'll** — 'I will' becomes 'I'll' — the apostrophe replaces the missing 'w' and 'i'.
2) **isn't** — 'is not' becomes 'isn't' — the apostrophe replaces the missing 'o'.
3) **you're** — 'you are' becomes 'you're' — the apostrophe replaces the missing 'a'.
4) **haven't** — 'have not' becomes 'haven't' — the apostrophe replaces the missing 'o'.
5) **I'm** — 'I am' becomes 'I'm' — the apostrophe replaces the missing 'a'.
6) **she's** — 'she is' becomes 'she's' — the apostrophe replaces the missing 'i'.
7) **We are** — 'We're' is a shortened form of 'We are' — the apostrophe replaces the missing 'a'.
8) **There is** — 'There's' is a shortened form of 'There is' — the apostrophe replaces the missing 'i'.
9) **had not** — 'hadn't' is a shortened form of 'had not' — the apostrophe replaces the missing 'o'.
10) **you will** — 'you'll' is a shortened form of 'you will' — the apostrophe replaces the missing 'w' and 'i'.

11) **Do not** — 'Don't' is a shortened form of 'Do not' — the apostrophe replaces the missing 'o'.
12) **could not** — 'couldn't' is a shortened form of 'could not' — the apostrophe replaces the missing 'o'.

Page 12 — Inverted Commas

1) **said** — This is a statement so 'said' is correct.
2) **asked** — This is a question so 'asked' is correct.
3) **said** — This is a statement so 'said' is correct.
4) **said** — This is a statement so 'said' is correct.
5) **asked** — This is a question so 'asked' is correct.
6) **asked** — This is a question so 'asked' is correct.
7) **"You can't play football in the garden," said Pete.** — The inverted commas go either side of the words that are spoken, and the second set need to go after the comma.
8) **"There's a hole in that bucket," noted Dave.** — The inverted commas go either side of the words that are spoken, and the second set need to go after the comma.
9) **"Can you mend my bike?" asked Kasra.** — The inverted commas go either side of the words that are spoken, and the second set need to go after the question mark.
10) **Aisha laughed and said, "I don't know where they are."** — The inverted commas go either side of the words that are spoken, and the second set need to go after the full stop.
11) **"Come back!" they shouted after him.** — The inverted commas go either side of the words that are spoken, and the second set need to go after the exclamation mark.
12) **Kirstie looked worried when she said, "Oh dear."** — The inverted commas go either side of the words that are spoken, and the second set need to go after the full stop.

Page 13 — Inverted Commas

1) **"You haven't tidied up!" shouted Dad.** — The inverted commas go either side of the words that are spoken, and the second set need to go after the exclamation mark.
2) **Bernard said, "I give up."** — The inverted commas go either side of the words that are spoken, and the second set need to go after the full stop.
3) **Rahim called, "Come on. Let's go!"** — The inverted commas go either side of the words that are spoken, and the second set need to go after the exclamation mark.
4) **"We can't find it anywhere," they said.** — The inverted commas go either side of the words that are spoken, and the second set need to go after the comma.
5) **let's** — The sentence should be '"Let's stroke the lambs," suggested Becky.' 'Let's' needs a capital letter because it's the first word of the speech.
6) **you're** — The sentence should be 'Ritu said, "You're not allowed to go alone."' 'You're' needs a capital letter because it's the first word of the speech.
7) **we're** — The sentence should be '"We're going to be late again," said Mum.' 'We're' needs a capital letter because it's the first word of the speech.
8) **hurry** — The sentence should be 'He called out, "Hurry up everybody!"' 'Hurry' needs a capital letter because it's the first word of the speech.
9) **our** — The sentence should be '"Our school uniform is horrid," I complained to Marieke.' 'Our' needs a capital letter because it's the first word of the speech.
10) **look** — The sentence should be 'Uncle Billy exclaimed, "Look! Those people are riding camels!"' 'Look' needs a capital letter because it's the first word of the speech.

Page 14 — Mixed Punctuation Questions

1) **hair,** — The sentence should be 'The old man had dyed his hair.' Sentences never finish with a comma.
2) **baby** — The sentence should be 'Baby Frieda learnt to walk.' Sentences always start with a capital letter.
3) **here?** — The sentence should be 'Get down here!' This sentence shows strong feelings so it should end in an exclamation mark.
4) **Quilt** — The sentence should be 'I sleep best when I have a feather quilt.' The word 'quilt' doesn't need a capital letter because it's in the middle of a sentence and it isn't a proper noun.
5) **play!** — The sentence should be '"Can I go out to play?" asked Ted.' There should be a question mark at the end of the speech because Ted is asking a question.
6) **"and** — The sentence should be 'Carlos threw the ball and yelled, "Catch this!"' The inverted commas should only be at the start of the speech.
7) **T** — Sentences always start with a capital letter. The sentence should be 'Two men swam out to the island.'
8) **"** — There should be a second set of inverted commas after the word 'yet?'. The sentence should be '"Are we nearly there yet?" I asked.'
9) **'** — There should be an apostrophe in 'It's' because it is a shortened version of 'It is'. The sentence should be 'It's nearly time to leave.'
10) **'** — There should be an apostrophe in 'Don't' because it is a shortened version of 'Do not'. The sentence should be 'Don't say that, Amy.'
11) **.** — There should be a full stop at the end of the sentence. The sentence should be 'Ritala took the book from the shelf.'
12) **,** — There should be a comma between 'football' and 'I' to separate two parts of the sentence. The sentence should be 'When we play football, I go in goal.'

Page 15 — Mixed Punctuation Questions

1) **"How long are we going for?" asked Hussein.** — There should be a set of inverted commas after 'for?' to show where the speech ends.
2) **Everybody was at Ben's party except Glenn, Sam and Jane.** — There should be a comma between 'Glenn' and 'Sam' to separate the names in the list.
3) **I like eating ice cream, pizza, salad and bananas.** — There should be a comma between 'pizza' and 'salad' to separate the items in the list.
4) **Before I go to school, I clean my teeth.** — There should be a comma after 'school' to separate the two parts of the sentence.
5) **"When are you going to tidy your room?" asked Dad.** — There should be a question mark after 'room' because Dad is asking a question.
6) **"Josephine and Hazel are my best friends," Archna explained.** — There should be a set of inverted commas at the start of the sentence to show that Archna is speaking.
7) **Their dad is an astronaut and he's going to the moon.** — There should be a full stop at the end of the sentence.
8) **Margaret's jacket is the one with the fur hood.** — There should be an apostrophe in 'Margaret's' to show that the jacket belongs to her.
9) **"Meita!" Lesley shouted up the stairs.** — There should be an exclamation mark after 'Meita' because Lesley is shouting.
10) **We're going on a school trip to Germany in the spring.** — There should be an apostrophe in 'We're' because this is a shortened version of 'We are'.
11) **Mum said, "I've got a surprise for you."** — There should be a full stop after 'you' because it is the end of the sentence.

12) **When I go running, I listen to music.** — There should be a comma between 'running' and 'I' to separate the two parts of the sentence.

Page 16 — Plurals

1) **girls** — 'girl' becomes 'girls' — words ending in 'l' add 's' to make the plural.
2) **boxes** — 'box' becomes 'boxes' — words ending in 'x' add 'es' to make the plural.
3) **ashes** — 'ash' becomes 'ashes' — words ending in 'sh' add 'es' to make the plural.
4) **glasses** — 'glass' becomes 'glasses' — words ending in 'ss' add 'es' to make the plural.
5) **peaches** — 'peach' becomes 'peaches' — words ending in 'ch' usually add 'es' to make the plural.
6) **wishes** — 'wish' becomes 'wishes' — words ending in 'sh' add 'es' to make the plural.
7) **boys** — 'boy' becomes 'boys' — words ending in a vowel and a 'y' add 's' to make the plural.
8) **valleys** — 'valley' becomes 'valleys' — words ending in a vowel and a 'y' add 's' to make the plural.
9) **jellies** — 'jelly' becomes 'jellies' — words ending in a consonant and a 'y' add 'ies' to make the plural.
10) **puppies** — 'puppy' becomes 'puppies' — words ending in a consonant and a 'y' add 'ies' to make the plural.
11) **chimneys** — 'chimney' becomes 'chimneys' — words ending in a vowel and a 'y' add 's' to make the plural.
12) **flies** — 'fly' becomes 'flies' — words ending in a consonant and a 'y' add 'ies' to make the plural.

Page 17 — Homophones

1) **too** — 'too' makes sense here — it means 'more than you would like'.
2) **two** — 'two' makes sense here — it is the word for the number 2.
3) **too** — 'too' makes sense here — it means 'more than you would like'.
4) **to** — 'to' makes sense here — it shows where they are going.
5) **piece** — 'piece' makes sense here — it means 'a bit' or 'a section'.
6) **peace** — 'peace' makes sense here — it means 'calm and quiet'.
7) **piece** — 'piece' makes sense here — 'all in one piece' is a phrase that means 'all together'.
8) **peace** — 'peace' makes sense here — it means 'calm and quiet'.
9) **their** — 'their' makes sense here — it means 'belonging to them'.
10) **their** — 'their' makes sense here — it means 'belonging to them'.
11) **they're** — 'they're' makes sense here — it is a shortened version of 'they are'.
12) **there** — 'there' makes sense here — it is a word used to show location.

Page 18 — Prefixes and Suffixes

1) **ness** — The word is 'illness'.
2) **ship** — The word is 'relationship'.
3) **ness** — The word is 'fitness'.
4) **ness** — The word is 'fairness'.
5) **ship** — The word is 'membership'.
6) **ship** — The word is 'partnership'.
7) **un** — The word is 'unpleasant'.
8) **dis** — The word is 'disagreed'.
9) **un** — The word is 'unwrap'.
10) **dis** — The word is 'disappear'.
11) **im** — The word is 'imperfect'.
12) **im** — The word is 'impossible'.

Page 19 — Awkward Vowels

1) **i** — The word is 'pain'.
2) **u** — The word is 'minutes'.
3) **e** — The word is 'forest'.
4) **o** — The word is 'mirror'.
5) **a** — The word is 'primary'.
6) **e** — The word is 'poem'.
7) **shield** — The rule is 'i before e except after c, but only when it rhymes with bee'. The 'ie' in 'shield' rhymes with 'bee', so it's spelt 'shield'.
8) **achievement** — Remember the rule: 'i before e except after c, but only when it rhymes with bee'. The 'ie' in 'achievement' rhymes with 'bee', so it's spelt 'achievement'.
9) **brief** — Remember the rule: 'i before e except after c, but only when it rhymes with bee'. The 'ie' in 'brief' rhymes with 'bee', so it's spelt 'brief'.
10) **ceiling** — Remember the rule: 'i before e except after c, but only when it rhymes with bee'. The 'ei' in 'ceiling' comes after 'c' and rhymes with 'bee', so it's spelt 'ei'.
11) **science** — Remember the rule: 'i before e except after c, but only when it rhymes with bee'. The 'ie' in science comes after 'c' but it doesn't rhyme with 'bee', so it's spelt 'ie'.
12) **niece** — Remember the rule: 'i before e except after c, but only when it rhymes with bee'. The 'ie' in 'niece' rhymes with 'bee', so it's spelt 'niece'.

Page 20 — Awkward Consonants

1) **k** — The word is 'knuckles'.
2) **h** — The word is 'white'.
3) **w** — The word is 'wrinkles'.
4) **k** — The word is 'knitting'.
5) **g** — The word is 'gnomes'.
6) **h** — The word is 'hours'.
7) **squirrels** — 'squirrels' is always spelt with a double 'r' in the middle.
8) **biting** — 'biting' is always spelt with one 't' in the middle.
9) **bubbles** — 'bubbles' is always spelt with a double 'b' in the middle.
10) **running** — A second 'n' is added to the word 'run' when the suffix 'ing' is added.
11) **waddles** — 'waddles' is always spelt with a double 'd' in the middle.
12) **hoping** — The 'e' is removed from the word 'hope' when the suffix 'ing' is added, but a second 'p' is not added.

Page 21 — Mixed Spelling Questions

1) **unhappy** — 'un' is the correct prefix to be added to the word 'happy'.
2) **correct** — 'correct' is always spelt with a double 'r' in the middle.
3) **ditches** — Words ending in 'ch' add 'es' to make the plural.
4) **knock** — 'knock' has a silent 'k' at the beginning.
5) **hiding** — The 'e' is removed from the word 'hide' when the suffix 'ing' is added.
6) **keys** — Words ending in 'ey' add 's' to make the plural.
7) **shadow** — 'shadow' has a 'w' at the end.
8) **cheerful** — The suffix 'ful' is always spelt with one 'l'.
9) **Tomorrow** — 'Tomorrow' has one 'm' and a double 'r'.
10) **plums** — The word 'plums' (meaning 'the fruit') isn't spelt with a 'b'.
11) **skies** — Words ending in a consonant before the 'y' add 'ies' to make the plural.

Answers

12) **aliens** — Remember the rule: 'i before e except after c, but only when it rhymes with bee'.

Page 22 — Mixed Spelling Questions

1) **freind** — 'freind' should be 'friend' — it follows the rule 'i before e except after c'.
2) **activitys** — 'activitys' should be 'activities' — words ending in a consonant before the 'y' add 'ies' to make the plural.
3) **court** — 'court' should be 'caught' — it is the past tense of the verb 'to catch'.
4) **rapper** — 'rapper' should be 'wrapper' — it has a silent 'w' at the beginning.
5) **ribons** — 'ribons' should be 'ribbons' — it has a double 'b' in the middle.
6) **lisened** — 'lisened' should be 'listened' — it has a silent 't' after the 's'.
7) **pensil** — 'pensil' should be 'pencil' — it has a 'c' in the middle.
8) **joly** — 'joly' should be 'jolly' — it has a double 'l' in the middle.
9) **peice** — 'peice' should be 'piece' — remember the rule 'i before e except after c, but only when it rhymes with bee'.
10) **pasing** — 'pasing' should be 'passing' — it has a double 's' in the middle.
11) **brekfast** — 'brekfast' should be 'breakfast' — it is made from the two words 'break' and 'fast'.
12) **torchs** — 'torchs' should be 'torches' — words ending in 'ch' often add 'es' to make the plural.

Page 23 — Alliteration and Onomatopoeia

1) **Betty bit butter batter** — The 'b' sound is used to form the alliteration.
2) **Summer season see sun** — The 's' sound is used to form the alliteration.
3) **Fiona found Flora's friend's feather** — The 'f' sound is used to form the alliteration.
4) **desperate dog ducked door** — The 'd' sound is used to form the alliteration.
5) **Lying log lazy ladybird laughed** — The 'l' sound is used to form the alliteration.
6) **Colin came collect clay** — The 'c' sound is used to form the alliteration.
7) **popped** — 'popped' is the best word to describe the noise a bottle top makes.
8) **cooing** — 'cooing' is the best word to describe the noise a dove makes.
9) **clunked** — 'clunked' is the best word to describe the noise a train makes.
10) **gulped** — 'gulped' is the best word to describe the noise you make when you drink quickly.
11) **slurped** — 'slurped' is the best word to describe the noise you make when you eat spaghetti.
12) **roared** — 'roared' is the best word to describe the noise an aeroplane makes.

Page 24 — Synonyms

1) **nice** — 'nice' is closest in meaning to 'kind'.
2) **risky** — 'risky' is closest in meaning to 'dangerous'.
3) **cheerful** — 'cheerful' is closest in meaning to 'happy'.
4) **loud** — 'loud' is closest in meaning to 'noisy'.
5) **hot** — 'hot' is closest in meaning to 'boiling'.
6) **breezy** — 'breezy' is closest in meaning to 'windy'.
7) **rapidly** — 'rapidly' is closest in meaning to 'quickly'.
8) **blanket** — 'blanket' is closest in meaning to 'quilt'.
9) **flowers** — 'flowers' is closest in meaning to 'plants'.
10) **afraid** — 'afraid' is closest in meaning to 'scared'.
11) **dirty** — 'dirty' is closest in meaning to 'filthy'.
12) **jacket** — 'jacket' is closest in meaning to 'coat'.

Page 25 — Antonyms

1) **messy** — 'messy' is opposite in meaning to 'neat'.
2) **under** — 'under' is opposite in meaning to 'above'.
3) **boy** — 'boy' is opposite in meaning to 'girl'.
4) **narrow** — 'narrow' is opposite in meaning to 'wide'.
5) **quiet** — 'quiet' is opposite in meaning to 'busy'.
6) **cheap** — 'cheap' is opposite in meaning to 'expensive'.
7) **hard** — 'hard' is opposite in meaning to 'soft'.
8) **light** — 'light' is opposite in meaning to 'heavy'.
9) **empty** — 'empty' is opposite in meaning to 'fill'.
10) **forget** — 'forget' is opposite in meaning to 'remember'.
11) **lose** — 'lose' is opposite in meaning to 'win'.
12) **handsome** — 'handsome' is opposite in meaning to 'ugly'.

Page 26 — Creative Writing

1) **many answers possible** — e.g. 'sorrowful' or 'gloomy'.
2) **many answers possible** — e.g. 'kind' or 'likeable'.
3) **many answers possible** — e.g. 'huge' or 'massive'.
4) **many answers possible** — e.g. 'scarlet' or 'crimson'.
5) **many answers possible** — e.g. 'tiny' or 'little'.
6) **many answers possible** — e.g. 'damp' or 'drenched'.
7) **many answers possible** — e.g. 'glances' or 'stares'.
8) **many answers possible** — e.g. 'smashing' or 'breaking'.
9) **many answers possible** — e.g. 'touched' or 'tapped'.
10) **many answers possible** — e.g. 'whistle' or 'sing'.
11) **many answers possible** — e.g. 'rushed' or 'sprinted'.
12) **many answers possible** — e.g. 'making' or 'building'.

Page 27 — Creative Writing

1) **many answers possible** — e.g. 'black' and 'fluffy'.
2) **many answers possible** — e.g. 'strict' and 'tall'.
3) **many answers possible** — e.g. 'wicked' and 'frightening'.
4) **many answers possible** — e.g. 'bright' and 'busy'.
5) **many answers possible** — e.g. 'noisy' and 'fun'.
6) **many answers possible** — You get one mark for each of the three characters or places you have used: a cat, a policeman, a witch, the seaside and a fairground. To get the other three marks your story needs to make sense, have a beginning, a middle and an end and contain at least 4 adjectives.

Page 28 — Non-Fiction Writing

1) **F** — The moon can't wink or sing so this sentence is from a fiction text.
2) **F** — A magical kingdom is not real so this sentence is from a fiction text.
3) **N** — This sentence is an instruction from a recipe so it's from a non-fiction text.
4) **N** — This sentence is telling the reader a fact about frogs so it's from a non-fiction text.
5) **F** — Monkeys can't speak so this sentence is from a fiction text.
6) **N** — This sentence is telling the reader a fact about the inventor of the telephone so it's from a non-fiction text.
7) **Turn** — The instruction should be 'Turn the light off in the living room.'
8) **Plug** — The instruction should be 'Plug in the radio to listen to the show at eight o'clock.'

9) **Fix** — The instruction should be 'Fix the picture to the wall in the hallway.'
10) **Take** — The instruction should be 'Take bus number six into town.'
11) **Go** — The instruction should be 'Go out of the building by the back door.'
12) **Leave** — The instruction should be 'Leave before the end of the party.'

Page 29 — Non-Fiction Writing

1) **many answers possible** — One idea is — Find your toothbrush and toothpaste. Squeeze a little toothpaste onto the toothbrush. Put the toothbrush under the tap to wet it. Put the toothbrush in your mouth and brush all your teeth. Spit out the toothpaste and rinse your mouth.

2) **many answers possible** — One idea is — Choose some wrapping paper. Put the present on the paper and cut around it, leaving plenty of space. Fold up the edges of the wrapping paper over the present. Use sticky tape to tape the edges together. Tie a ribbon around the present.

Pages 30-34 — Assessment Test 1

1) **B** — In the recipe it says "100 g of caster sugar".
2) **C** — The first instruction in the recipe is "Separate the yolks from the egg whites".
3) **D** — In the recipe it says that the "mixture will get stiffer as you do this". "stiffer" means 'to thicken'.
4) **A** — In the recipe it says to "whisk the cream until it is thick".
5) **B** — The blackcurrant juice is added in step 7, straight after the instruction to "Beat the egg yolks for a few seconds, and then add them to the egg white and cream mixture."
6) **D** — In the recipe it says "put it in the freezer for at least 12 hours".
7) **D** — In the recipe it says to take your ice cream out of the freezer "about ten minutes beforehand to make it easier to serve".
8) **E** — "Beat" is closest in meaning to 'Mix'. Both words mean 'to stir'.
9) **B** — This means that the mixture is thick enough to hold its shape.
10) **C** — "beforehand" is closest in meaning to 'earlier'. Both words mean 'to do something before'.
11) **A** — 'arrive' is correct because it completes the phrase 'didn't arrive'.
12) **B** — 'turned' is correct because it is in the past tense and it agrees with the noun 'people'.
13) **C** — 'had' is correct because it is in the past tense and completes the phrase 'had almost reached'.
14) **A** — 'when' is correct because it introduces the second part of the sentence.
15) **D** — 'over' is the correct word to complete the phrase 'fell over'.
16) **D** — 'there' should be 'their' — these are homophones and 'their' is correct because it shows who the leader belongs to.
17) **A** — 'Making' should be 'making' — the 'e' is dropped from the word 'make' when the suffix 'ing' is added.
18) **A** — 'whether' should be 'weather' — these are homophones and 'weather' is correct because the sentence is about weather conditions.
19) **E** — 'mudy' should be 'muddy' — a 'd' is added when the suffix 'y' is added to the word 'mud'.
20) **E** — 'sails' should be 'sales' — these are homophones and 'sales' is correct because it means 'selling things at a lower price'.
21) **E** — 'could'nt' should be 'couldn't' — it is a shortened version of 'could not' and the apostrophe takes the place of the missing letter, in this case, the 'o' of 'not'.
22) **A** — The inverted commas should be before the word 'When' because this is the start of the speech.
23) **A** — 'crumpet's' should be 'crumpets' — this word is a plural so it doesn't need an apostrophe.
24) **E** — There shouldn't be inverted commas at the end of the sentence as the speech finishes after the word 'running'.
25) **A** — There shouldn't be a comma after 'Ramana'.

Pages 35-39 — Assessment Test 2

1) **C** — In the passage it says they were on a "long lakeside walk".
2) **D** — In the passage it says the "long, hot afternoon was slowly turning cooler" which shows that it was the late afternoon.
3) **A** — In the passage it says that their campsite is "at the other end of the lake".
4) **D** — In the passage it says that running "wasn't easy as they had rucksacks on their backs".
5) **E** — The only item that isn't mentioned is a picnic blanket.
6) **B** — In the passage it says that they had to "step around a muddy puddle" — "step around" is another word for 'avoid'.
7) **E** — In the passage it says "they had made it" which means both of them caught the ferry.
8) **A** — "in despair" means 'to have given up hope'.
9) **C** — "retrace their steps" means 'walk back the way they had come'.
10) **D** — "to their relief" means they were pleased to see the ferry.
11) **C** — 'see' is correct because it completes the phrase 'we went to see'.
12) **E** — 'get' is correct because it is in the present tense and agrees with the pronoun 'I'.
13) **B** — 'to' is the correct word because it completes the phrase 'next to'.
14) **E** — 'eat' is correct because it completes the phrase 'will eat'.
15) **D** — 'that' is correct because it goes with 'The house'.
16) **A** — 'pencill' should be 'pencil' — there is only one 'l' at the end.
17) **A** — 'creem' should be 'cream' — the long 'ee' sound can be spelt 'ea'.
18) **B** — 'circcus' should be 'circus' — there's only one 'c' in the middle.
19) **C** — 'freinds' should be 'friends' — the rule is 'i before e except after c'.
20) **E** — 'hairdressor' should be 'hairdresser' — the ending is 'er'.
21) **A** — There should be a capital letter at the start of the sentence.
22) **B** — 'Station' doesn't need a capital letter — it's not at the start of the sentence and it isn't the name of a particular person or place.
23) **E** — There should be a full stop at the end of the sentence rather than a question mark.
24) **B** — 'daffodil's' should be 'daffodils' — this is a plural so it doesn't need an apostrophe.
25) **A** — 'Dont' should be 'Don't' — this is a shortened version of 'Do not' so there should be an apostrophe between the 'n' and the 't' to represent the missing letter.

Pages 40-44 — Assessment Test 3

1) **E** — In the letter Nisha says that she lives "close to the seaside".
2) **D** — Nisha says she thought she would "swim in the sea everyday".
3) **D** — Nisha wonders "if it is ever hot in England".
4) **C** — Nisha says "Mum made me wear so many clothes that I couldn't move my arms properly".
5) **B** — Nisha says they sledged "down a hill".
6) **A** — At the end of the letter Nisha says "I will send you some photographs".
7) **D** — Nisha says "I played with the children next door".

Answers

8) **B** — Nisha says "I have missed you", which shows that she hasn't seen Badal for a long time.
9) **B** — The word "shocked" means 'surprised'.
10) **A** — "glittering" means 'sparkling'.
11) **E** — 'to' is correct because it completes the phrase 'next to'.
12) **E** — 'them' is the correct pronoun because it goes in place of the noun 'the coins'.
13) **D** — 'as' is correct because it completes the phrase 'as well as'.
14) **C** — 'into' is correct because it shows how Billy reached the hotel lobby.
15) **B** — 'he' is the correct pronoun because it goes in place of the noun 'Billy'.
16) **E** — 'frosen' should be 'frozen' — the root word is 'freeze' with a 'z'.
17) **D** — 'becuse' should be 'because' — there is an 'a' after the 'c'.
18) **E** — 'holliday' should be 'holiday' — there is only one 'l'.
19) **A** — 'carfully' should be 'carefully' — the suffix 'fully' has been added to the word 'care'.
20) **D** — 'parth' should be 'path' — it is not spelt with an 'r'.
21) **E** — There should be a full stop at the end of the sentence.
22) **A** — 'over' should have a capital letter because it is at the start of a sentence.
23) **E** — There should be a full stop before the inverted commas after the word 'mine'.
24) **D** — There shouldn't be a capital letter on the word 'roundabout' — it isn't at the beginning of a sentence and it isn't the name of a particular person or place.
25) **B** — 'holiday's' should be 'holidays' — this is a plural so it doesn't need an apostrophe.

Pages 45-49 — Assessment Test 4

1) **C** — The passage starts with "Long, long ago".
2) **B** — In the passage it says "the cot was overturned", and "overturned" means 'knocked over'.
3) **A** — "Alarmed" means 'worried'.
4) **C** — When the Prince finds that his baby son is missing he thinks that the dog has attacked him.
5) **C** — The Prince realises that the dog didn't hurt the baby and he feels guilty for sending the dog away — "filled with regret" means 'feels guilty'.
6) **A** — In the passage the wolf is described as "enormous" — this means 'huge'.
7) **A** — The dog protected the baby from the wolf so he is not 'evil'.
8) **E** — "fury" means 'rage'.
9) **B** — "banished" means 'sent away'.
10) **C** — "companion" means 'friend'.
11) **B** — 'drank' is correct because it is in the past tense and goes with the noun 'Tim'.
12) **A** — 'take' is the correct word to complete the phrase 'should take'.
13) **D** — 'running' is the correct word to go with 'children' and to complete the phrase 'running around'.
14) **C** — 'asked' is correct because it is in the past tense and goes with the noun 'his aunt'.
15) **D** — 'his' is correct because it shows that the head belongs to 'Tim'.
16) **B** — 'leeked' should be 'leaked' — the root word is 'leak' which means 'to let through water'.
17) **E** — 'pairs' should be 'pears' — these are homophones and 'pears' is correct because it is a type of fruit.
18) **A** — 'stackked' should be 'stacked' — it is spelt with only one 'k'.
19) **C** — 'suger' should be 'sugar' — the ending is 'ar'.
20) **B** — 'new' should be 'knew' — these are homophones and 'knew' is correct because it is the past tense form of 'to know'.
21) **B** — There should be a question mark after 'hat' because it is a question.
22) **E** — 'doesnt' should be 'doesn't' — the apostrophe shows that the letter 'o' is missing between the 'n' and the 't'.
23) **C** — There doesn't need to be a comma before the word 'and'.
24) **E** — There should be a full stop at the end of the sentence.
25) **A** — 'december' should be 'December' — this is a proper noun so it needs a capital letter.

Pages 50-54 — Assessment Test 5

1) **C** — In the passage it says that squirrels build their nests "in the folds of a tree trunk".
2) **B** — In the passage it says that "Baby squirrels are called kittens".
3) **B** — In the passage it says that squirrels "spend time in autumn storing food".
4) **A** — In the passage it says that their tail "helps the squirrel to balance as it moves through the trees".
5) **D** — In the passage it says red squirrels "are about 12 weeks old when they develop their own teeth".
6) **C** — In the passage it says that "grey squirrels were brought over from America".
7) **D** — The only food that isn't mentioned is berries.
8) **C** — "majority" means the same as 'most'.
9) **A** — "rare" means the same as 'uncommon'.
10) **B** — "occasionally" means 'sometimes'.
11) **D** — 'invited' is the correct word to complete the phrase 'I was invited'.
12) **D** — 'saw' is correct because it is in the past tense and agrees with 'I'.
13) **A** — 'in' is the correct word to complete the phrase 'in their garden'.
14) **C** — 'written' is the correct word to complete the phrase 'had written'.
15) **A** — 'had' is the correct past tense form of the verb 'to have' and agrees with the noun 'Everyone' to complete the sentence.
16) **B** — 'poped' should be 'popped' — there is a double 'p' in the middle.
17) **E** — 'flys' should be 'flies' — the ending is 'ies' when 'fly' is plural.
18) **B** — 'which ' should be 'witch' — these are homophones and 'witch' is correct because it means 'a woman who works magic'.
19) **E** — 'puddel' should be 'puddle' — the ending is 'le'.
20) **D** — 'chillyest' should be 'chilliest' — the 'y' from the word 'chilly' becomes an 'i' when the suffix 'est' is added.
21) **D** — There shouldn't be any inverted commas after the word 'man' because the speech has already finished.
22) **C** — The question mark should be inside the inverted commas.
23) **B** — There shouldn't be a comma after the word 'active' because the two parts of the sentence do not need separating.
24) **C** — 'theres' should be 'there's' — it is a shortened version of 'there is' so there needs to be an apostrophe in place of the missing letter.
25) **C** — 'Castle' does not need a capital letter because it is not at the beginning of a sentence and it isn't the name for a particular person or place.

Pages 55-59 — Assessment Test 6

1) **D** — Father William is described as "old" and "fat", with "very white" hair — 'overweight' means the same as "fat".
2) **B** — The young man is asking Father William whether it is a good idea for him to stand on his head when he is so old.
3) **C** — Father William says that he stands on his head "again and again".

4) **D** — Father William says that when he was young he "feared it might injure the brain".
5) **E** — Father William says that he is sure that he doesn't have a brain so he won't be hurt by standing on his head.
6) **A** — The young man is surprised Father William can do somersaults because he is "uncommonly fat".
7) **B** — The young man is asking why Father William did a somersault at the door.
8) **A** — "In my youth" is closest in meaning to 'in my childhood'. 'Youth' and 'childhood' both mean 'in your younger years'.
9) **C** — "replied" means the same as 'answered'.
10) **E** — In this context, "mentioned" means the same as 'said'.
11) **A** — 'knew' is the correct word because it is the past tense of the verb 'to know' and it agrees with the pronoun 'I'.
12) **C** — 'where' is the correct word here because the speaker is asking about the location of the jumper.
13) **C** — 'mice' is the correct plural of 'mouse'.
14) **D** — 'quickly' is the correct option because it describes the verb 'turned'.
15) **D** — 'worst' is the correct option because it describes the noun 'morning'. It is correct because it means 'most bad'.
16) **A** — 'listend' should be 'listened' — the suffix 'ed' has been added to the word 'listen'.
17) **E** — 'woodden' should be 'wooden' — the suffix 'en' has been added to the word 'wood'.
18) **B** — 'night' should be 'knight' — these are homophones and 'knight' is correct because it means 'a soldier'.
19) **E** — 'brake' should be 'break' — these are homophones and 'break' is correct because it makes sense in the phrase 'break free'.
20) **C** — 'wear' should be 'where' — these are homophones and 'where' is correct because the sentence is talking about location.
21) **D** — 'frog's' should be 'frogs' — it is a plural so it doesn't need an apostrophe.
22) **A** — There shouldn't be a comma after 'passed' because the sentence doesn't need separating there.
23) **E** — This is a question so it needs a question mark at the end of the sentence.
24) **A** — There should be some inverted commas before 'He's' because it is the start of the speech.
25) **E** — There shouldn't be a comma between 'bitter' and 'cold'.

Pages 60-64 — Assessment Test 7

1) **A** — In the passage it says that the trees looked different because "it was growing dark".
2) **E** — Tariq doesn't crawl in the passage.
3) **B** — In the passage Tariq wonders if the sound of the wind is actually "something stalking him through the woods". "stalking" means the same as 'following'.
4) **E** — Tariq charges "straight into the dense bushes".
5) **A** — In the passage it says that the woods "slapped his face" but not a person.
6) **A** — Tariq comes into the campsite "with a crash".
7) **C** — Tariq's father is cooking dinner when Tariq gets back to the tent.
8) **E** — "clawed" is closest in meaning to 'scratched'.
9) **A** — "dense" is closest in meaning to 'thick'.
10) **B** — "prevent" is closest in meaning to 'stop'.
11) **B** — 'live' is correct because it is in the present tense and agrees with the noun 'brothers'.
12) **E** — 'are' is correct because it is in the present tense and agrees with the noun 'brothers'.
13) **B** — 'their' is the correct word because it shows the tree house belongs to them.
14) **A** — 'them' is correct because it refers to the three brothers.
15) **A** — 'because' makes the most sense in this sentence.
16) **E** — 'buy' should be 'by' — these are homophones and 'by' is correct because it shows how they picked the vegetables.
17) **E** — 'here' should be 'hear' — these words are homophones and 'hear' is correct because it is a verb which means 'to listen'.
18) **B** — 'seeside' should be 'seaside' — this is a compound word made from the words 'sea' and 'side'.
19) **E** — 'wite' should be 'white' — it has a silent 'h' in it.
20) **D** — 'waist' should be 'waste' — these are homophones and 'waste' is correct here because it means 'throw away'.
21) **E** — The word 'Teacher' doesn't need a capital letter.
22) **E** — There should be a question mark at the end of this sentence.
23) **A** — There shouldn't be a comma after the word 'growling'.
24) **E** — There shouldn't be an apostrophe at the end of 'eyes' because it is a plural.
25) **C** — There shouldn't be a question mark after 'football' because it is not a question — there should be an exclamation mark.

Pages 65-69 — Assessment Test 8

1) **C** — In the passage it says that "everyone who lived in a country which was part of the Roman Empire had to obey Roman laws".
2) **E** — The text does not mention markets.
3) **A** — There is nothing in the text about the name of the city of Rome.
4) **D** — In the passage it says that the Romans built roads to transport goods "quickly and directly".
5) **B** — In the passage it says that the soldiers had "lots of equipment like helmets, shields and spears".
6) **E** — Hospitals aren't mentioned in the text.
7) **D** — The Roman Empire included North Africa but not South Africa.
8) **E** — "talented" is closest in meaning to 'skilful'.
9) **A** — "remained" is closest in meaning to 'stayed'.
10) **A** — "at its peak" means 'when it was most powerful'.
11) **D** — 'escape' is correct because it completes the phrase 'Bob could not escape'.
12) **D** — 'heavily' makes the most sense in this sentence.
13) **E** — 'together' is correct because it shows how Jo rubbed her hands.
14) **B** — 'to' is correct because it completes the phrase 'to try'.
15) **A** — 'put' is correct because it complete the phrase 'to put'.
16) **C** — 'sandwhiches' should be 'sandwiches' — there is no 'h' after the 'w'.
17) **D** — 'biggist' should be 'biggest' — the suffix should be 'est'.
18) **E** — 'warter' should be 'water' — there is no 'r' after the 'a'.
19) **E** — 'smocke' should be 'smoke' — there is no 'c' in 'smoke'.
20) **A** — 'foxs' should be 'foxes' — 'es' is added to the word 'fox' to make it plural.
21) **D** — There doesn't need to be a comma after the word 'goldfish'.
22) **C** — 'play's' should be 'plays' — it is the verb in this sentence and isn't a shortened version of anything so it doesn't need an apostrophe.
23) **E** — There shouldn't be any inverted commas after the word 'stairs'.
24) **E** — There should be a full stop after 'assembly' because it is the end of the sentence.
25) **C** — The word 'mountains' doesn't need a capital letter because it isn't at the start of a sentence and it isn't the name of a particular place or person.

Answers